Developing Research in Teacher E

Good teacher education, informed by relevant research, is judged by policy makers and practitioners alike to be central to increasing the quality of schooling in many countries of the world. Yet, in the UK, research on teacher education is often acknowledged to be less well developed than other areas of educational research and to be over-determined by education policy. It has also been accused of a lack of rigour and of being atheoretical. A further challenge in developing good research in teacher education is that new teacher educators commonly face the challenge of moving into academic work without relevant research skills and the ready capacity to produce high quality research outputs. For these reasons, then, strengthening research in and on teacher education is high on educational agendas in the UK.

This book examines the exact nature of these challenges in teacher education and the initiatives arising to address them in different settings across the four nations of the UK. The central theme of all the chapters is how to build 'research capacity' so that teacher education can contribute more strongly to the improvement of schooling, as well as becoming a high quality, research-informed enterprise in its own right. The insights will be valuable to teacher educators around the world.

This book was published as a special issue of the *Journal of Education for Teaching*.

Ian Menter is Professor of Teacher Education at the University of Glasgow, UK, a Special Professor at the University of Nottingham and is an Academician of the Academy of Social Sciences.

Jean Murray is Professor of Education at the University of East London, UK, and an Associate Director of Escalate (the Higher Education Subject Centre for teacher education).

Developing Research in Teacher Education

Edited by
Ian Menter and Jean Murray

Routledge
Taylor & Francis Group
LONDON AND NEW YORK

First published 2011
by Routledge
2 Park Square, Milton Park, Abingdon, Oxon, OX14 4RN

Simultaneously published in the USA and Canada
by Routledge

711 Third Avenue, New York, NY 10017

Routledge is an imprint of the Taylor & Francis Group, an informa business

First issued in paperback 2012

This book is a reproduction of the *Journal of Education for Teaching*, vol. 35, issue 4. The Publisher requests to those authors who may be citing this book to state, also, the bibliographical details of the special issue on which the book was based

Typeset in Times New Roman by Taylor & Francis Books

British Library Cataloguing in Publication Data
A catalogue record for this book is available from the British Library

ISBN13: 978-0-415-59486-8 (hbk)
ISBN13: 978-0-415-65796-9 (pbk)

Disclaimer
The publisher accepts responsibility for any inconsistencies that may have arisen in the course of preparing this volume for print

Contents

Notes on Contributors

Vivienne Baumfield is professor of pedagogy, policy and innovation in the Faculty of Education at the University of Glasgow and co-director of the International Educational Consultancy. She is also the University's International Regional Champion for South and Central Asia.

Anne Campbell is a visiting professor at Leeds Metropolitan University in the Carnegie Faculty of Sport and Education. She has researched in the areas of practitioner research and professional learning, through action research, evaluation, and fictional writing and narrative approaches.

Donald Christie is a professor in the Department of Childhood and Primary Studies at the University of Strathclyde. His research interests include: children's social development; collaborative learning; the professional development of teachers and other caring professionals; and community of enquiry as a model for educational research. He was the convenor of the AERS Learners, Learning and Teaching Network, funded from 2004–2009. He is a former president of the Scottish Educational Research Association and is a member of the BERA Council.

Susan M.B. Davies is a senior lecturer in the School of Education Studies and Social Inclusion at Trinity University College, University of Wales. She was the chair and co-ordinator of the Welsh Education Research Network.

Yvonne Dewhurst lectures in the School of Education, the University of Aberdeen, Scotland. She has worked in a range of educational roles and presented several international keynote addresses and conference papers. For the past 16 years she has managed national conferences for teachers. Her research interests are in situated student teacher learning and home economics.

Peter Gilroy is professor emeritus at Manchester Metropolitan University (MMU) and holds visiting chairs at Roehampton and Southampton Universities. He was until recently the Director of Research and Enterprise at MMU and responsible for the university's 2008 RAE return. He has published widely in the field of professional development and is currently working on a book examining research audit processes.

Archie Graham graduated in geography and qualified and worked as a primary teacher before joining the Northern College, Aberdeen. Since the merger of Northern College with the University of Aberdeen he has worked as a lecturer on the PGDE programme and is currently the PGDE deputy programme director, Learning and Teaching.

Donald Gray is a senior lecturer and director of research for the Scottish Teachers for a New Era initiative at the University of Aberdeen. He was a science teacher before joining the Scottish Council for Research in Education followed by posts at Strathclyde University, Humboldt University, Berlin and the University of Aberdeen.

Ian Hextall is senior research fellow at Roehampton University. He taught for many years in higher education at Goldsmiths College, and also at the London Institute, University of Kent and South Bank University. He is currently pursuing research interests in the impacts of ICT initiatives in schooling and, also, the dynamics of the Building Schools for the Future programme.

Moira Hulme is a lecturer in educational research and co-director of the Chartered Teacher programme at the University of Glasgow. She contributes to the faculty Pedagogy, Policy and Practice research group and is the project coordinator of Research to Support Schools of Ambition (2006–2010), funded by the Scottish government.

Marion Jones is professor of teacher education at Liverpool John Moores University. She is involved in the teaching and supervision of doctoral students and provides support for developing researchers in teacher education. Her own research is primarily concerned with issues related to initial teacher education, induction and continuing professional development with a particular focus on mentoring.

Gllian Kirkpatrick was a primary teacher prior to joining the Northern College of Education Aberdeen and subsequently the School of Education of Aberdeen University where she was director of Undergraduate Programmes before relocating to Singapore in 2008.

Ruth Leitch is a senior lecturer and former head of the School of Education, Queen's University Belfast. She is a member of BERA Council and the Northern Ireland academic representative on the Strategic Forum for Research in Education and a member of the Northern Ireland Education Research Forum.

Lindsay MacDougall was a primary teacher before becoming a lecturer in education at the University of Aberdeen in 2001. Lindsay teaches on the PGDE and BEd programmes and her research interests are in the areas of classroom learning and teaching and the professional development of teachers including teacher as researcher.

Pat Mahony is emertius professor of education at Roehampton University. She convened Network 10 within the European Educational Research Association between 2002 and 2005 and is a past chair of the University Council for the Education of Teachers (UCET) Research Committee. Her research focuses on teacher education and social justice.

Olwen McNamara is a professor of teacher education and development at the University of Manchester, UK. Her research interests are in professional learning and mathematics education. She publishes widely in these fields and her books include: *New teacher identity and regulative government* (Brown and McNamara, 2005, New

York: Springer) and *Practitioner research and professional development in education* (Campbell, McNamara and Gilroy, 2004, London: Sage).

Ian Menter is a professor in the Department of Curriculum Studies and was deputy dean of the Faculty of Education at the University of Glasgow from 2005-09. He is the chairperson of the Research Committee of the Universities Council for the Education of Teachers and represents the Scottish Educational Research Association on the Council of the European Educational Research Association. He was a member of the AERS Executive Committee. His research interests lie in policy making and teacher education, with a particular interest in education policy in the 'post-devolution' UK.

Jean Murray is professor of education and research leader in the Cass School of Education at the University of East London. She is an associate director of ESCalate and a BERA Special Interest Group convenor. Her research focuses on teacher educators, research capacity building and pedagogies for teacher education.

Sandra Nicol graduated in 1978 with a degree in sociology and gained a masters in education in 2000. She taught in the primary sector for 15 years, joining staff at University of Aberdeen in 2006. She is currently working with final-year BEd students and is programme director for Chartered Teacher.

Graeme Nixon is a lecturer in education, specialising in religious, moral and philosophical studies. Research interests include the emergence of philosophy in Scottish religious education and mindfulness in education. Graeme teaches student teachers in both primary and secondary sectors, as well as delivering development training for existing teachers.

Fran Payne is a senior research fellow in the School of Education, University of Aberdeen. Her research interests lie in curriculum innovation in secondary schools, the use of ICT in teaching and learning, teachers' continuing professional development, and in supporting practitioner research.

Richard Procter worked for the Centre for Applied Research in Educational Technologies at the University of Cambridge and for the Teaching and Learning Research Programme at the Institute of Education, University of London. He is now a freelance consultant, pursuing his interests in new technologies to improve teaching and learning across phases, support for e-research and capacity building.

Grant Stanley is a post-doctoral research assistant and module leader/lecturer for the MRes programme at Liverpool John Moores University. His research interests are located in the research capacity building of both teachers and initial teacher educators and the generation and dissemination of research findings to these professionals through collaborative projects with psychology researchers that bridge the pure–applied research divide.

Howard Tanner is reader in education at Swansea Metropolitan University (SMU) where he trains mathematics teachers for secondary schools. He is director of the Centre for Research in Education at SMU and an executive member of the Welsh Educational Research Network. His research interests include: teacher education, dialogic pedagogies, ICT and mathematics education.

NOTES ON CONTRIBUTORS

Karl Wall is a lecturer in the Department of Psychology and Human Development at the Institute of Education, University of London. His research interests include teacher–pupil communication, special educational needs and pedagogic training and practice.

INTRODUCTION

Capacity building in teacher education research

Ian Menter[a] and Jean Murray[b]

[a]*Department of Curriculum Studies, University of Glasgow, Glasgow, UK;* [b]*Cass School of Education, University of East London, London, UK*

In these times of accountability and audit, it should come as no surprise that there has been a great concern – some might say obsession – with 'capacity building'. This is a term that crops up in a huge variety of settings, for example, in business and commerce, in voluntary organisations and charities, in warfare and defence and, not least, in education and specifically in educational research. This Special Issue of *JET* is concerned with aspects of capacity and capacity building in teacher education research. It focuses on the peculiar context of the United Kingdom, where we have recently been through the Research Assessment Exercise (RAE) (see Gilroy and McNamara in this issue) and are even now in preparation for its successor, the Research Excellence Framework (REF) in 2013. However, we believe the general issues raised here about research-capacity building in teacher education are of significance in many contexts around the world, not least in continental Europe (see, *inter alia*, Erixon Arreman 2008; Lunenberg, Ponte and Van de Ven 2007), North America (see, *inter alia,* Cochran-Smith and Zeichner 2006) and Australia (Reid 2009).

This Special Issue emerged from a session held during the annual conference of the Universities' Council for the Education of Teachers (UCET) in Birmingham, UK, in November 2008. That session brought together teacher education researchers from across the four nations of the UK – England, Northern Ireland, Scotland and Wales – to explore what was happening within each jurisdiction. What emerged very strongly from the presentations and discussion was that there is considerable variation between the four nations, but also, in all cases, there are some very major challenges facing the research communities. Four of the eight papers in this issue emerge directly from the conference (Murray et al.; Leitch; Christie and Menter; Tanner and Davies), but they are complemented by four others, which provide, respectively, an overview of the RAE (Gilroy and McNamara) and three examples of particular approaches to research capacity development (Hulme et al.; Gray et al.; Wall et al.).

At the outset, it is important to acknowledge that the term 'capacity building' is not without some difficulty. In her paper, Leitch discusses some of the assumptions that are frequently made in discussions on this topic. Capacity may be taken to relate to some or all of the following: the range of skills available; the research infrastructure (funding, facilities, etc.); the numbers of experienced and/or qualified researchers. Furthermore, there is little point in having substantial capacity, if the quality of that capacity is at a low level. Problems with the terminology and the relationship between capacity and quality were key topics of discussion at the first meeting of the UK

Strategic Forum for Research in Education (SFRE) (Pollard 2008). While all of the papers in this issue are concerned with capacity building they each relate to a particular context, either nationally or institutionally and the conceptualisation of capacity building varies accordingly.

Notwithstanding these considerations of terminology, there have been several serious attempts to support the development of research capacity in education within the UK over recent years. The Teaching and Learning Research Programme (TLRP) has operated across all four nations since 2001, with a total investment of approximately £40 million. The main part of the programme is now finished although a strand relating to technology-enhanced learning continues. In Scotland, the Applied Educational Research Scheme (AERS) had an investment of £2 million over a five-year period, 2003–2008. More recently in Wales, the Welsh Educational Research Network (WERN) was funded at a much lower level and over a short time-span of one year (with a second year's extension now coming to a close). The recent establishment of a UK-wide Strategic Forum for Research in Education (SFRE) is seeking to harness some of these developments and to ensure that the researchers, policy-community and education practitioners work together to sustain what has been achieved (Pollard 2008).

All of these national capacity building schemes, which are referred to in more detail in papers in this issue (see Wall et al., Christie and Menter, Tanner and Davies, respectively), result at least in part from concern about the need to improve the quality of educational research, to make it more productive in relation to policy and practice and to ensure that there is a strong and sustainable infrastructure. This is not the place to carry out an evaluation of the extent to which these aims have been achieved, but rather to reflect on the extent to which they have promoted the development specifically of teacher education research.

Teacher education research is an especially important part of the wider field of education research, we contend, for the following reasons. First, the majority of academic staff in UK university education departments have significant responsibility for the delivery of teacher education programmes. Indeed for many staff it is seen as their primary function, sometimes as quite separate from other activities, including research. This can result in the creation of a 'dual economy' within faculties of education (Munn and Baron 2008). Second, there is a strong lobby to maintain – or in some cases to introduce – a research dimension directly into teacher education, so that the work of teaching can be clearly acknowledged as research-informed, research-oriented or research-based. Third, and in spite of the two previous points, in the UK as elsewhere, teacher education research is a relatively new and relatively underdeveloped sub-field of education research (Zeichner 1999; cited in Cochran-Smith and Zeichner 2006, 755). Furthermore, it was suggested by the 2008 RAE Education sub-panel (see Gilroy and McNamara in this issue) that there was little evidence of significant development in this sub-field in the UK between 2001 and 2008.

So, to what extent have the capacity building schemes contributed to the development of teacher education research? The TLRP supported over 100 projects during its first three major phases. A review of the outcomes that related to teacher learning and development in particular was undertaken by Jephcote and Menter for a major TLRP dissemination event held late in 2008. They reviewed just the eight projects that appeared to have a particular connection to this theme (see Menter and McNally forthcoming, for a summary). Although this research provided important and significant insights, the actual impact of this work on policy and practice is difficult to detect at present, although the evaluations that are being undertaken may throw further light on this. The AERS approach in Scotland also included a range of work concerned with teacher development and that is addressed in the paper by Christie and Menter that follows. It is very early to be making judgements about the contribution and impact of WERN in Wales to teacher education research specifically, although the indications from the paper by Tanner and Davies are that some teacher education colleagues have successfully exploited opportunities to develop their research skills.

The one project that very directly aims to improve research capacity within teacher education is that described in the paper by Murray et al. As the authors say, this was designed as a pilot project of one year's duration to be carried out within one English region. We write as the period of funding is coming to an end and can report that there does appear to have been a significant development for many colleagues across the region. Whether this can be sustained after such a short and intense period of activity is a big question. There can be little doubt that any sustained development will require a major investment of funding and in the current economic climate, it is difficult to be optimistic that this will be forthcoming. Even relatively small-scale investment to maintain initiatives such as the Teacher Education Group (TEG) resource (see the paper by Wall et al.) is difficult to secure. Indeed many of the papers in this issue take a pessimistic view about the future funding of education research in general, in spite of the enthusiasm and efforts that are reported in many of the articles.

Elsewhere, colleagues, including ourselves, have written in brief about the history of teacher education research in the UK and have offered an analysis of the characteristics of this research (Menter et al. forthcoming; see also Wall et al. in this issue). There is a paucity of longitudinal and of quantitative work. On the positive side there is clearly a great deal of developmental research taking place that is helping to inform local practices in teacher education and some imaginative use of qualitative and interpretative methods.

An important distinction is sometimes made between research *on* teacher education and research *in* teacher education. As has already been indicated, there is much research carried out by teacher education practitioners into their own working practices and experiences. Indeed such work can often be described as practitioner research, some of it of a very reflexive nature (see Gray et al. in this issue). The recognition that many teacher educators are 'second career researchers' who have significant induction and training needs is a relatively recent phenomenon (Boyd, Harris and Murray 2007; Harrison and McKeon 2008; Murray 2008). But research may also be carried out on teacher education, where the researchers are external to the immediate field of practice and the TEG bibliography (Wall et al. in this issue) includes some such work.

This distinction is also reflected in the range of approaches to capacity building that are covered in the articles in this issue. Four papers offer an overview of developments within each nation, but they also show network-based (e.g. AERS) and project-based (e.g. WERN) approaches. Research training of various sorts can also be seen as a key element (for example in AERS) and particular resources, such as the TEG bibliography may play a key part in this (as in the elements of knowledge exchange and mediation within the TERN project). But there are also ways in which forms of developmental research or practitioner research may be incorporated into teacher education programmes (Scottish Teachers for a New Era, as described by

Gray et al.) or school development (Schools of Ambition, as discussed by Hulme et al.). Perhaps the single thing that emerges most strongly from all of the work reported here is the emphasis on collaboration and co-operation, in various forms of what has been called a 'social practices' model of capacity building (Rees et al. 2007; Munn 2008). Another theme that can be detected at many points in these papers is the significance, complexity and variability of the relationships between research, policy and practice and their respective 'communities' which are sometimes intersecting and overlapping.

It is our hope that the work reported here will provide insights that can inform the pursuit of further progress in this relatively new sub-field of education research. Improvements in the capacity and quality of this body of research are, we contend, essential to the healthy future of teacher education in universities, colleges and schools in the UK and the rest of the world.

Acknowledgements

We are very grateful to the authors who submitted papers for this Special Issue. They have had to work within a very tight timescale to submit and revise their papers in order that such a topical volume has emerged on time. We are also very grateful to our team of reviewers, half of them from the UK and half from overseas, who also worked at great speed to meet what might, in other circumstances, have been deemed unreasonable deadlines.

References

Boyd, P., K. Harris, and J. Murray. 2007. *Becoming a teacher educator: Guidelines for the induction of newly appointed lecturers in Initial Teacher Education.* York, UK: ESCalate, HEA.

Cochran-Smith, M., and K. Zeichner, eds. 2006. *Studying teacher education: The report of the AERA Panel on Research and Teacher Education.* Washington, DC: AERA and Lawrence Erlbaum Associates.

Erixon Arreman, I. 2008. The process of finding a shape: Stabilizing new research structures in Swedish Teacher Education (2000–2007). *European Educational Research Journal* 7, no. 2: 321–33.

Harrison, J., and F. McKeon. 2008. The early research career development of beginning teacher educators – a case study approach. Paper presented at the European Educational Research Conference, 10–13 September, in Gothenburg, Sweden.

Lunenberg, M., P. Ponte, and P. Van de Ven. 2007. Why shouldn't teachers and teacher educators conduct research on their own practices? An epistemological exploration. *European Educational Research Journal* 6, no. 1: 13–24.

McNally, J. and I. Menter. 2009, in press. Editorial. *Teaching and Teacher Education* 25, no. 7: 141–3.

Menter, I., M. Hulme, M. Jones, J. Murray, A. Campbell, I. Hextall, P. Mahony, R. Procter, and K. Wall. Forthcoming. Teacher education research in the UK: The state of the art. *Swiss Revue of Educational Research.*

Munn, P. 2008. BERA presidential address: Building research capacity collaboratively: Can we take ownership of our future? *British Educational Research Journal* 34, no. 4: 413–30.

Munn, P., and S. Baron. 2008. Research and practice. In *Scottish Education.* 3rd ed., ed. T. Bryce, and W. Humes, 864–72. Edinburgh: University of Edinburgh.

Murray, J. 2008. Teacher educators' induction into higher education: Work-based learning in the micro communities of teacher education. *European Journal of Teacher Education* 31, no. 2: 117–33.

Pollard, A., ed. 2008. Quality and capacity in UK education research. Report of the first meeting of the UK's Strategic Forum for Research in Education, October 16–17, in Harrogate, UK. http://www.sfre.ac.uk/wp-content/uploads/2009/03/report-final-march-2009.pdf

Rees, G., S. Baron, R. Boyask, and C. Taylor. 2007. Research-capacity building professional learning and the social practices of educational research. *British Educational Research Journal* 33, no. 5: 761–79.

Reid, J. 2009. Issues in consolidating research in teacher education: An Australian perspective. Paper presented at the American Educational Research Association Annual Conference, April, in San Diego, CA.

A critical history of research assessment in the United Kingdom and its post-1992 impact on education

Peter Gilroy and Olwen McNamara

[a]*Professor Emeritus, Manchester Metropolitan University, Manchester, UK;* [b]*School of Education, University of Manchester, Manchester, UK*

This paper presents a critical overview of the way in which higher education institutions (HEIs) in the UK have had their research activity subject to review. There have been six such reviews to date, the first two carried out by the Universities Grants Committee and, from 1992, by its replacement, the four UK higher education (HE) funding bodies (HE Funding Council for England, HE Funding Council for Wales, the Scottish HE Funding Council and the Department for Employment and Learning in Northern Ireland). The paper provides a broad outline of the key elements of the process, focusing on the two more recent research reviews and their impact on the subject of education, with the references providing specific detail for those interested in the minutiae of the reviews.

> I hope I shall make it plain: though things one has taken for granted all one's life, like the flowing of the tide, are hard to explain to those who do not know the meaning of high tide or low… (O'Brian 1997, 105)

Introduction

We open this paper with a brief description of the historical background to the research audits that have become such a key feature of university life in the UK over the last 20 years or so. The first two such audits were, as we shall show, relatively benign affairs and, as with all subjects in the university, research funding for education was barely affected by them. It was only with the third audit in 1992, when the polytechnics were transformed into 'new' universities, that the research audit really began to bite. The results of the audit produced noticeable disparities in the allocation of research funding, especially as these impacted on research funding for education. It is at this point that the research audits became a major issue for the research community, including education.

University research funding pre-1992

Prior to 1986 every university in the UK received a research grant as part of their block grant formula from the Universities Grants Committee (UGC) funded in relation to their student numbers, 'irrespective of the volume or quality of its research' (Newall

2003, 144). Obviously the larger the university the greater its block grant, regardless of its research quality (however such quality might be measured). The political, and possibly social, context the UK found itself in by the 1980s created a position whereby this state of affairs could no longer be accepted, with selectivity based on performance replacing the more *laissez faire* attitude of the UGC. Within this framework education, as a subject for research, was funded like any other subject in the university.

1986: the first Exercise

The first UK-wide Research Assessment Exercise (RAE) took place in 1986. Known as the Research Selectivity Exercise (RSE) it was carried out by the UGC. The Higher Education Funding Council for England (HEFCE) states that:

> The primary function of the RAE ratings was to inform the funding bodies' allocation of grant for research, reflecting the established government and funding bodies policy that these resources should be allocated according to research quality. The exercise also had important roles in providing both public information and quality assurance for public expenditure on research in higher education. (HEFCE 2004, 4)

However, at the time in question it seemed more a *quid pro quo* for releasing more research money to the sector and was a very light touch exercise. For some at least, the RSE was in effect an exercise which would allow a university to 'account for the public funding it receives' by identifying performance indicators, that is publications (Bence and Oppenheim 2005, 4). Given the economic circumstances of the 1970s, with for example a four-fold increase in the price of oil, the public sector as a whole was under pressure from successive governments to show value for money, and the university sector was not exempt from this pressure to account for the funding it received.

This viewpoint is confirmed by Tapper, who argues that selectivity in research in the UK has a history that goes back to at least 1965, something the UGC tried to manage by a light touch approach. However, given the political context of the 1980s the UGC found itself on the horns of a dilemma created by the then Conservative government:

> Thus the emergence of the RAEs has to be placed in the context of the increased political scrutiny of higher education. The Thatcher government was determined to control public funding while at the same time securing 'better value for money'. The UGC was in the unenviable position of either resisting government pressure and risking its demise or responding positively and alienating segments of the academic community. (Tapper 2007, 189)

The UGC decided to turn its back on its natural 'community' and opted for the latter option, whilst subsequently being replaced with the Universities Funding Council (UFC). It was the UFC which also launched the 1989 Exercise, and those that followed were the joint responsibility of the four UK higher education (HE) funding bodies, representing England, Northern Ireland, Scotland and Wales.

Bence and Oppenheim (2005) argue, with Cave et al. (1997; cited in Bence and Oppenheim 2005), that the 1986 Exercise was an attempt to re-work a very general indicator of performance into a specific performance indicator (PI). Making use of Cuenin's (1986; cited in Bence and Oppenheim 2005) distinction, they stress that a PI, unlike a simple indicator (such as a numerical figure, which is more or less an objective descriptor), 'imply a point of reference… or comparator, and are therefore relative rather than absolute in character' (Bruce and Oppenheim 2005, 5). It is worth noting at this point that the education press ignored this aspect of the PIs and persisted (and persist still) in translating them into simple indicators which then allows for a hierarchical league table of higher education institutions (HEIs) to be created, based superficially on their research profile.

Research funding was allocated by reference to the RSE's results, and so HEIs found themselves in a situation whereby it could be argued that the Exercise was 'determining rather than measuring the way research is conducted in universities' (Lee and Harley 1998; cited in Bence and Oppenheim 2005, 6). The process was far from clear, hence the call for greater transparency.

The 1986 RSE process, launched by the UGC without any consultation with the sector, made use of a very light touch approach, and required universities merely to complete a questionnaire which included just five exemplars of the research outputs from each department (identified as 39 'cost centres'). What should be noted here is that, although some university-wide data were required, the emphasis was away from funding *universities'* research to funding *departmental/cost centre* research within a university. There were no stigma attached to non-inclusion in such a tiny data set (and from personal experience one author of the paper can vouch for the fact that there was no reward attached to having one's work included in the return). The returns were considered by the UGC's subject groups, and 'rated against a variety of scales and standards' (Phillimore 1989; cited in Bence and Oppenheim 2005, 10). With many criticisms of the process as one that 'lacked consistency, anonymity and comprised incomplete and inaccurate data collection' (Bence and Oppenheim 2005), in particular the 'glaring absurdity' (Tapper 2007, 191) of the differing grading scales for subjects, it was inevitable that it had to change.

1989: the second Exercise

The 1989 Exercise, launched by the UFC, was also relatively low-key. There was widespread consultation which resulted in a number of significant changes. The 50 cost centres were replaced with 152 Units of Assessment (UoAs), with a five-point rating scale introduced replacing the three-point scale of 1986. Academics in the universities had only to identify what they considered to be their two finest publications produced between January 1984 and December 1988, and other information on post-graduate research students and research income was required. The previous subject committees of the UGC were replaced with 70 peer reviewer panels and the anonymity of their membership was dropped after the Exercise had been completed.

The UFC's own evaluation of the Exercise concluded that 'publication data was found to be unreliable, and where it was reliable, it said nothing about the quality of the output' (UFC 1989, para. 23; cited in Bence and Oppenheim 2005, 14). The problem faced then, and which possibly remains now, is 'what to collect and what measurements to use' (Bence and Oppenheim 2005, 14), to which could be added how it (whatever the 'it' might be) can be judged. Moreover, as UoAs (more often no more than subject departments by another name) were now what the Exercise focussed on, as opposed to a university's overall provision, senior managers had been provided with a tool to judge, however crudely, the performance of these units. This Exercise, therefore, continued the process of highlighting the performance, or lack of it, of individual subject domains.

1992: the third Exercise

The 1992 Exercise was launched against a background of the transformation of the polytechnics into 'new' universities through the Further and Higher Education Act of that year. Unlike the pre-1992 universities (often referred to as the 'old' universities), who were funded for both research and teaching, the 'new' universities' funding regime was focussed entirely on teaching. As a result the assumption that all staff were carrying out research had to be changed, with 'the concept of "research active"... introduced' (Evidence 2006, 14).

For a subject with a heavy practitioner focus, such as education, the introduction of the distinction between applied and blue-skies research was significant, although apparently 'hardly any submissions made such a distinction' (Evidence 2006, 13). There were 72 UoAs, each research active staff had to identify two publications and provide information on all their outputs for the period, this being checked through an audit process. A five-point grade scheme was used by the expert panels (grades 1–5, where 1 represented little or no research 'excellence').

Almost inevitably the 'old' universities garnered the majority of the research funding (91% – Bence and Oppenheim 2005, 16) and those with the lowest grade received no funding whatsoever. The educational press used elements of the RAE data to produce league tables which, although statistically unsound, were in the public domain and so became another element of the process to which universities had to adjust (*Times Higher Education Supplement* 2001, 7).

Education (UoA 71) received 86 submissions from across the UK, 32% of which were rated 4 or 5 as they were considered to demonstrate evidence of some internationally excellent work. At the other end of the scale 13% of submissions were considered to show virtually no evidence of nationally excellent work and, as a consequence, received no funding. Although all of these latter submissions were from post-1992 universities, some optimism about the fledgling post-1992 research cultures might have appeared justified at this stage. Overall, they comprised 48% of the total submissions to UoA, 71 and 73% demonstrated national excellence in over half their outputs, with one, the University of the West of England, having national excellence in all their outputs (see Table 1).

The level of research activity in the devolved administrations of the United Kingdom varied. In Scotland, all seven institutions returned were awarded some funding, three were graded 4 or 5 and four 2 or 3. In Wales the six institutions returned were all graded 2 or 3. Of the three institutions submitted in Northern Ireland two were graded 3 but the third failed to demonstrate any evidence of national level of work, so received no research funding.

Table 1. Disaggregation of Education Unit of Assessment (UoA) 1992 outcomes by type of institution.

1992 rating	1	2	3	4	5	Institutions submitting to UoA 71
Post-1992 institutions	11	20	9	1	0	41
Pre-1992 institutions	0	3	16	14	12	45
All institutions	11	23	25	15	12	86

A retrospective review of the impact of the 1992 RAE on HEIs (HEFCE 1997) undertaken by HEFCE, and drawing on a number of sources, identified early evidence of what were to become continuing debates in the education sector regarding the developing RAE culture. Most significant was an underlying fear that the RAE was 'distorting professionally related subjects (education, business and management, economics)' (HEFCE 1997, para. 114) and in particular was valuing theoretical work more highly than research which had a focus on practice. The general problem of how research and practice could be most effectively integrated in fields such as education also appeared as an issue. Concern was also expressed as to the possible bifurcation of research and teaching activities in the pre-1992 institutions as a result of selectivity in research funding.

1996: the fourth Exercise

The 1996 Exercise again was preceded by a consultation exercise which led to a number of changes in the subsequent Exercise. Research active staff had to be identified, with each offering four outputs as well as indicators of 'peer esteem'. The previous five-point grading scale was expanded to seven points (1, 2, 3b, 3a, 4, 5 and 5*), with no funding allocated to grades 1 and 2 and a non-linear approach to the allocation of funds (e.g. a UoA rated at 5*, defined as research of 'international excellence', would receive four times the funding of a UoA rated 3b [Tapper 2007, 193]).

Thus, this Exercise introduced a policy of very high research selectivity. Bearing in mind that the next Exercise would see more of the 'new' universities joining the scramble for research funding it is no surprise to see HEFCE warning that 'unless there is extra money from Government to reward any continuing general improvement in research ratings in the 2001 RAE, funding will have to be more selective' (HEFCE 2000, 2). There were 69 UoAs, panels were appointed through nominations by various bodies and panel criteria were made public. Again, this resulted in a single RAE grade for a UoA. It once more produced an extensive critique and the thoroughgoing 'Fundamental Review of Research Policy', whose report was the basis for further consultation. Unfortunately this consultation was organised via an electronic questionnaire, whose questions were somewhat restrictive in the responses that were available to those completing it. (For more detail of the Review's finding see Evidence [2006, 44–7].)

RAE 1996 saw a 20% increase in the number of institutions in the UK returning to education, now identified as 'UoA 68' (see Table 2). Although the grade profile of the outcomes shows a slight increase in the number of highly rated (4–5*) submissions (from 27 in 1992 to 30 in 1996), only two institutions were awarded the new 5* rating, King's College London and the Institute of Education at London University. Again a degree of optimism about the research capacity of post-1992 institutions could be justified. They had been given some development funding in the lead up to the 1992 Exercise, although there was no explicit policy to induct them into the process by, for example, involving their staff as peer assessors on the panels or providing them formative feedback (HEFCE 1997). Yet the post-1992 sector demonstrated an increase of more than 40% in institutional submissions in 1996, to the extent that they outnumbered the pre-1992 sector for the first time.

In terms of funding all pre-1992 university departments and 21 of the 58 post-1992 institutions (who were rated 3 and over) received some funding, but the non-linear

Table 2. Disaggregation of Education Unit of Assessment (UoA) 1996 outcomes by type of institution.

1996 rating	1	2	3b	3a	4	5	5*	Institutions submitting to UoA 68
Post-1992 institutions	13	24	14	7	0	0	0	58
Pre-1992 institutions	0	0	6	10	17	11	2	46
Total	13	24	20	17	17	11	2	104

funding model meant that the post-1992 institutions, none of which were rated 4–5*, garnered relatively little funding in real terms.

The result of the 1996 research review of the UK HEI sector demonstrated a sustained or enhanced research culture. In Scotland of the 10 institutions this time returned, all but two received funding and three achieved grades 4–5. In Wales six institutions were returned and four received funding but only one achieved a grade 4. In Northern Ireland two institutions were returned and both were graded 4.

The burgeoning of the nascent research cultures did not, however, come at a propitious time in the education sector. Education researchers were involved in a bitter debate about the quality of educational research, and most particularly its relevance to schools and improving educational outcomes (see, for example, Hargreaves 1996a, 1996b, 1997; Hammersley 1997), triggering the commissioning of two reports (Tooley and Darby, 1998; Hillage et al., 1998). A systematic mapping and analysis of 1996 RAE education submissions data was also undertaken (Kerr et al. 1998) to assist HE funding councils in planning research themes of strategic importance to shape the nature of the proposed programme of pedagogic research, which was to become the £30+ million Teaching and Learning Research Programme (TLRP) (2000–2009).

Kerr et al.'s (1998) analysis of the 1996 RAE education submissions concluded:

(1) Three overarching themes predominated: education (encompassing teaching, learning and subject-based enquiry); education policy; and education management.
(2) The predominant focus and organisation of research was through subject studies.
(3) The range of external funding varied enormously and unevenly across institutions and between years. Some two-thirds of institutions in receipt of external funding received up to £200,000 (in each year of the submission period). The remaining one-third received between £200,000 and over £2 million. The largest external source of funding was UK central and local government bodies (46%), followed by charities (19%) and research councils (13%).
(4) The level of external funding was closely related to RAE rating, and increased in step with the rating achieved. Institutions achieving rating levels 3b and below received considerably less funding than those at 3a and above; thus, the 'old' universities received considerably more funding than the 'new'.

The predominant focus on subject studies had implications for the proposed programme of pedagogic research which, it was envisaged, would fund generic research with practical applications, rather than subject-specific. Bassey and Constable (1997) also identified a tendency to divergence in the research focus associated with the RAE rating of education departments. Teacher/school/child issues, teaching/learning issues, disciplines in educational settings and methodology were all associated with highly rated departments. Teacher education and curriculum issues were disproportionately associated with lower-rated departments.

2001: the fifth Exercise

The 2001 RAE operated in much the same way as the 1996 Exercise, although there were some notable differences, especially regarding the allocation of funding. Research outputs' quality *per se* is what was supposed to be judged, definitions were provided to distinguish research from scholarship and it was stressed that 'the assessment process is based on peer review and is not mechanistic' (HEFCE 1999, para 1.2). There was initially the same seven-point grading system with funding originally intended to be allocated, in a non-linear way, to all but the three lower grades (1, 2 and 3b).

Subsequently, although Sir Howard Newby, as chief executive of HEFCE, had previously assured the sector that UoAs with grades 3a and above would be funded, it was announced that the 3a grade (defined as research of national excellence and 'showing evidence of international excellence') would not be awarded funding, an announcement that caused an outburst of anger by the sector. However, an additional grade of 6* was created (where a 1996 5* UoA had achieved the same or higher research grade whilst returning the same or more staff as in 1996). A limited number of seven so-called 'emerging subject areas', such as drama and the performing arts, but not education, and which had been awarded a grade 3a or below could bid for research capability funding so as to develop their research profile (HEFCE 2003b).

This was a major exercise whereby the publications of approximately '50,000 researchers in 2598 submissions from 173 HEIs' were examined (HEFCE 2008, 1). RAE 2001 was undoubtedly a watershed for the education sector and the overall picture was extremely disheartening. The total number of submissions to UoA 68 was reduced by around 20% from its 1996 high. Table 3 maps the outcome of the 2001 RAE against its two predecessors and shows an apparently encouraging increase, both in number (from 27 to 30 to 33, respectively) and relative proportion (from 31% to 29% to 40%, respectively), of education departments rated highly (4–5*). The total number of active researchers entered in those departments had, however, remained relatively static throughout the three Exercises, as a result of increasing selectivity within institutions attempting to maximise their research income (Bassey 2002). The impact of internal selectivity was also noted in the Education Panel Report, together with the significantly lower proportions of submissions graded 1 and 2: this, it was conjectured, was a result of departments not funded in 1996 deciding not to resubmit (Higher Education and Research Opportunities [HERO] 2001). Only two institutions, this time the Universities of Bristol and Cardiff, were rated 5* and as a result no education departments attained the new 6* designation.

In terms of capacity building and finance the impact of the RAE was quite simply disastrous for the sector. The *Demographic review of the UK social sciences* (Mills et al. 2006) conducted post-RAE 2001 found education was significantly different

Table 3. Trends of the outcomes of Research Assessment Exercises (RAEs) 1992–2001.

<table>
<tr><th>Grade</th><th>1</th><th>2</th><th>3b</th><th>3a</th><th>4</th><th>5/5*</th><th>Total</th></tr>
<tr><td>1992 RAE
(Grade 1 not funded)</td><td>11</td><td>23</td><td colspan="2">25</td><td>15</td><td>12</td><td>86</td></tr>
<tr><td>1996 RAE
(Grades 1 and 2 not funded)</td><td>13</td><td>24</td><td>20</td><td>17</td><td>17</td><td>13</td><td>104</td></tr>
<tr><td>2001 RAE
(Grades 1, 2, 3b and 3a not funded)</td><td>1</td><td>8</td><td>22</td><td>19</td><td>19</td><td>14</td><td>83</td></tr>
</table>

from other social science disciplines. In terms of research activity education had the lowest proportion of staff entered in the 2001 RAE, just 42% compared with an average of 64% in other social sciences. As a sign of the times the oldest university School of Education in the UK, in the pre-1992 University of Liverpool, which gained a grade of 3b, was earmarked for closure in part because of its perceived weak research base, as defined by the RAE. Here the RAE can be seen as operating as a management tool for identifying departments/UoAs whose poor research performance was a justification for closure, irrespective of other elements of their contribution to the university's mission. In terms of funding only 40% of the 83 education submissions received funding (those rated 4–5*) and for nearly 60% of those (the 4-rated institutions) in England at least the funding was minimal.

The outcome of RAE 2001 across the devolved administrations and government office regions of the UK was again disappointing for education. In Scotland only six of the HEIs were returned; four were rated 4, one 3a and one 3b. This triggered a £2 million research capacity building initiative (2002–2007) by the Scottish Education Funding Council and the Scottish Executive Education Department which funded the Applied Educational Research Scheme (AERS) (2004–2009), reported in detail later in this issue. In Wales five departments were returned of which one was rated 5*, three others were rated 3a and one was rated 2. Indirectly this outcome profile was instrumental in the development of the Welsh Educational Research Network, which again is reported in detail later in this issue. In Northern Ireland two departments were returned, one rated 4 and one 3a. Within England too, research production was significantly located in certain regions, with high densities in London and the Midlands and low densities in the east, south-east and north-west (Lawn and Furlong 2007).

In terms of overall capacity, whilst research was clearly still widely distributed across institutions 'with some small pockets of high quality and strategically important research taking place in many "non-elite" universities' (Furlong 2004, 2), the impact of the process of increasing selectivity on the post-1992 sector was devastating (see Table 4); the proportion submitting was down nearly 40% from its 1996 level. Only one, Manchester Metropolitan University, received any funding. More than 50% of education department staff were now employed in institutions that received no core research funding and about 34% of the total research active staff submitted to the RAE were now in departments that received no core research funding (Oancea 2004b). Dadds and Kynch (2003), in research commissioned by the British Educational Research Association, calculated that 80% of teachers were now trained in those non-research funded departments.

Table 4. Disaggregation of Education Unit of Assessment (UoA) 2001 outcomes by type of institution.

2001 rating	1	2	3b	3a	4	5	5*	Institutions submitting to Education (UoA 68)
Post-1992	0	8	19	8	1	0	0	36
Pre-1992	1	0	3	11	18	12	2	47

Oancea (2004a, 2004b) also demonstrated other differences between those education departments that received core research funding and those that did not. First, in terms of proportion of staff entered as research active this was on average almost 70% in research-funded departments compared to 35% in non-research-funded departments. Second, in terms of education research grant income (from government bodies, research councils, charities and European research project funding), research-funded departments attracted 78% of the total UK grant income compared with 22% in non-research-funded departments. Third, in terms of research audience and focus, research-funded departments focussed their research activity slightly more towards other researchers and policy makers, whereas non-research-funded departments reported a slightly higher proportion of their research directed towards the teacher audience; in so doing the latter were fostering a research culture which 'favours considerations of use and strong links with the teaching profession (with a view to development)' (Oancea 2004, 5).

HEFCE published a series of post-Exercise overview reports for each UoA. The Education Panel Overview Report identified a need for more approaches that made use of advanced quantitative methodologies and for education to play an active and significant role in methodological innovation. They also signalled the need for more 'blue skies' research, recourse to a wider range of funding bodies and more links between teaching and learning in the compulsory and post-compulsory sectors, and particularly further education and interdisciplinary links.

Although HEFCE claimed that 'The RAE is the principal means by which institutions assure themselves of the quality of the research undertaken in the HE sector' (HEFCE 2008, 1), they were well aware of the many criticisms of the RAE 2001 (HEFCE 2004, 4). Consequently, once again this Exercise spawned a review and consultation. As Evidence (2006) points out, the title of this review is significant, as Sir Gareth Roberts was commissioned by the four funding councils to produce not a simple review of the RAE 2001 but of 'Research Assessment' *per se*. Despite this wider remit the conclusion was that the RAE 2001 had, with some caveats, confirmed the 'centrality of expert [peer] review' to any such process, explicitly rejecting other performance indicators (HEFCE 2003a, para. 15).

2008: the sixth Exercise

RAE 2008 developed still further the 2001 approach. All outputs (four per person, with certain exceptions) were supposed to be read by the Panel members (and Panels now included international members who were intended 'as practising researchers' to 'bring an international perspective to… the quality profiles' [HEFCE 2007, 3]), but the key difference was the production of a quality profile which no longer allowed for individuals to be judged. The quality profile comprised three elements, research outputs, research environment and esteem indicators, all of which would be given a numerical grade on a five-point scale (unclassified, 1*, 2*, 3* and 4*). Elements of the profile would be weighted differently, depending on the subject panels' perception of their relative importance, this weighting varied dramatically in some cases, such that the research outputs' percentage could be as low as 50% of the profile, or as high as 70%, with the research environment varying from 20% to 5% (HEFCE 2005, 32).

One would have thought that such variety would make it difficult, if not impossible, to produce league tables, especially those that compared the results of this Exercise with its predecessors'. Not only was any comparison of subject against subject within the 2008 RAE suspect, given this variation, but any comparison with the results of the previous Exercise would in particular not be comparing like with like (with the exception of the eventual allocation of funds, announced in March 2009). However, these were not concerns that prevented a new round of league tables being produced (see for example, *Times Higher Education Supplement* 2008, 28–30, which includes another version of the table produced by Lancaster University, or the *Guardian* 2008).

Part way through the Exercise there was a worrying intervention by the Labour government. Roberts had claimed, with some justification, that the RAE 2001 'enabled funds to be concentrated in those departments best able to produce research of the highest quality' (HEFCE 2003a, para. 12). It was clear that the government, and especially the Treasury, were keen to see this concentration develop still further. The 2003 White Paper published barely two years after the formation of the Department for Education and Skills (DES) contained an implied criticism of the results of the RAE 2001, and what appeared to be an alarming interference with the autonomy of universities to decide their own mission by giving HEFCE more funding to allocate to 6* subject areas so as to make 'a clear distinction between the strong and the strongest' (DES 2003, 23) and thus allow for 'steering non-research-intensive institutions towards other parts of their mission, and rewarding them properly for it' (26). This produced intense lobbying by the sector and it is now clear that for the time being at least this 'steering' has been rebuffed, with HEFCE (unlike its predecessor, the UGC, in 1986) having the courage to keep faith with its academic community.

As this Exercise was drawing to its close there was a second attempt by the government to interfere with the process. It was perhaps their frustration with the lack of any radical alternative to academics judging academics that led the then Chancellor of the Exchequer, now prime minister, in an addendum to his Budget of 2006 to assert that the RAE 2008 should be replaced with a metrics-based system – and this less than 18 months before the RAE submission date (Her Majesty's Treasury 2006).

As one would expect this intervention produced an outburst of opposition from HEIs who had committed considerable resources to preparing for the RAE 2008. Eventually the proposal was partially withdrawn, being re-worked to allow for a metrics exercise of the science, technology, engineering and mathematics (STEM) subjects to be piloted alongside the RAE 2008, which is currently in its reporting stage. However, it is worth noting that the allocation of funds was, for HEFCE at least, based on a principle of 'funding research of the highest quality wherever and in whatever discipline it is found' while at the same time 'protecting the position of science subjects' (HEFCE 2009, 1), so some trace of the political interference in the process remains.

Table 5. Mapping of 2008 grade-quality descriptors against that of Research Assessment Exercises 2001/1996.

Year	None of national excellence	Less than two-thirds of national excellence	More than two-thirds of national excellence	Internationally recognised	Internationally excellent	World leading
2008	0	1*		2*	3*	4*
1996/2001	1	2 3b	3a 4	5	5* (6*)	

The introduction of the quality profile makes comparison between RAE 2001 and RAE 2008 outcomes in education difficult. Table 5 makes an attempt to map the grades of the two previous RAEs against the grade quality descriptors of RAE 2008 and demonstrates very clearly the significant leap it represents in terms of quality expectations.

Education (UoA 45) was now a sub-panel of Panel K, along with psychology and sports-related subjects. Eighty-one departments and 1903 research active staff were returned to UoA 45 along with 7146 outputs. Staff and outputs were down 15% and 20%, respectively, on the 2001 levels, although education was still overall fourth in terms of departments returned and seventh in terms of number of research active staff. The sector displayed considerable instability with only 80% of the 2008 submissions having returned to education in 2001 and a significant number of departments entering very small proportions of staff (30% with less than 10 and 70% with less than 20).

Overall about 80% of outputs were assessed to be of international standard (2* and above) and of these 40% were internationally excellent or better (3* and above) and 11% world-leading (4*). Table 6 shows the range of quality profiles ordered by grade point average (calculated with a weighting 4:3:2:1:0), together with the median, quartiles and arithmetic mean (a mean adjusted by volume of staff entered has also been given) (Brown, 2009).

The devolved administrations again varied. Scotland, perhaps as a result of its previous research capacity building, demonstrated considerably more robustness in terms of capacity, returning eight institutions and 267 (Category A) staff, putting it

Table 6. Unit of Assessment profiles (reproduced from Brown 2009).

Percentiles	4*	3*	2*	1*	0	GPA
Highest	35	30	25	10	0	2.90
5th percentile	25	35	30	10	0	2.75
Upper quartile	10	40	35	15	0	2.45
Median	5	25	40	25	5	2.00
Lower quartile	0	25	30	40	5	1.75
95th percentile	0	5	20	35	40	0.90
Lowest	0	0	15	55	30	0.85
Mean	8	23	33	27	9	2.00
Staff-adjusted mean	15	28	33	19	5	2.29

Note: GPA, grade point average.

back up to its 1996 level after a considerable down-turn in 2001. In Wales six institutions returned a total of 41 staff which represented a further down-turn, even after excluding the previously 5*-rated department at Cardiff which was on this occasion returned to an alternative UoA. In addition, half the institutions demonstrated no world-leading, and virtually no internationally excellent work. In Northern Ireland three institutions and 39 staff were returned, demonstrating a sustaining of previous levels of research capacity (HERO 2008).

The subject overview report (HERO 2008, 4) also noted 'significant improvements in some departments in post-1992 HEIs, with a few being amongst the best submissions in the Unit of Assessment'. Forty-two post-1992 universities entered in 2008, representing a 17% increase from 2001; of these 18 (43%) returned at least 5% of world-class outputs, of which five returned 10% world-class outputs and one, Manchester Metropolitan University, returned 20%.

There was also a significant broadening of the field reflecting a policy-led emphasis on integrated children's services. Some areas such as leadership and management and teacher education were less strongly represented than previously; notably the latter was identified by Bassey and Constable (1997) as a key focus of non-funded departments in 1996. The report from user members of the sub-panel expressed concern about the lack of school-based subject-specific research, which had also been noted as very strong in the 1996 RAE.

An overall improvement in research environment was evident with a quarter of returns having been judged to be at least internationally excellent in 50% of returns. The report, however, noted of the 7000 research students recorded less than 4% were funded by the Office of Science and Technology/research councils. Overwhelmingly the external research income of £316 million came from government (£182 million, amounting to nearly 60% of the total), followed by research funding councils (£55 million), charities (£37 million) and European Union funding (£18 million). The proportion of government funding was noted by the user members of the sub-panel as of interest and this had also been expressed as a concern of the 2001 Education Panel in their report. A plea was also made by users to disaggregate the total into government and regional development funding. Targeted research funding through Department for Children, Schools and Families research centres, TLRP and AERS was said to have impacted strongly at a national level on the research capacity building enterprise 'but many departments with world leading outputs had received little or no large-scale funding' (HERO 2008, 4).

Despite this apparently very positive result overall, education came a depressing sixty-fourth out of 67 UoAs in terms of percentage of internationally excellent and world-leading quality indicators. Only 14 out of 81 departments were at or above their institutional average (Brown 2009).

Conclusion

In terms of the research audit process as a whole, it is fair to say that after 1986, in addition to becoming ever more selective and resource intensive, subsequent exercises in HEFCE's view became 'gradually more transparent, comprehensive and systematic' (HEFCE 2008, 1), if only to ensure that academics remained on-side with the process. That is, the consultations could be seen as a process of learning from mistakes while ensuring that the process had legitimacy. Those responsible for designing and running the process had also gradually moved from bowing to government pressure to resisting it more or less effectively. The consultation process that is currently reporting in preparation for the launch of the next RAE, which will be phased in between 2010 and 2014, is focussed tightly on whether it is possible to use some form of bibliometrics to replace the expensive and time-consuming panel approach to judging research activity. At present the view of Evidence (2006) appears to be holding sway, especially in the social sciences, namely:

> …the system needs to retain expert review as a core element in the assessment process. It is clear that, even when encouraged to think more radically about possible assessment techniques, researchers across a wide range of subject disciplines retain a fundamental faith in international systems based on expert review by peers. (Evidence 2006, 11)

For the subject education the process has been a far from happy one. Education, the *Demographic review of the UK social sciences* (Mills et al. 2006) observed, was distinctive in a number of ways: it was the second largest discipline (with around 5000 staff compared to an average of less than 2000 in the other social science disciplines) and its staff had the oldest age profile (around 50% were aged over 50). Lawn and Furlong (2007) in a review of the social organisation of research conducted after RAE 2001 noted that 'as a field, educational research is not simply large, it is also very diverse and highly complex. It encompasses a wide range of substantive topics and theoretical perspectives… and employs multiple methodologies and practices' (Lawn and Furlong 2007, 57). They also observed that education research was no longer confined to education departments, with more and more research into education being undertaken outside universities, and as a result may have changed in form and purpose. Furthermore, they conclude that:

> …research in universities appears to be producing diverse forms, from a combination of mission and funding, which will have effects on career, subjects of study and audience, and which suggest that a single field of research will be hard to sustain. (Lawn and Furlong 2007, 68)

For teacher education the growing disconnection between departments receiving research funding and those in receipt of no such funding, but still responsible for working with teachers on initial and professional development programmes, is deeply worrying. This concern is particularly significant given the impending shift in the government's targeting of strategic funding for teacher development towards master's-level study and the consequent demands this will make on the research skills of the teacher education workforce. When one adds to this initiative the concurrent development of Post Graduate Certificates of Education carrying on average 60 master's-level credits and the aspiration to make teaching a master's-level profession the fact that so many staff and departments will have been identified as non-research active (in RAE terms) is a major concern. It would seem that either these master's programmes are to be taught by staff who are apparently not research active, or they are only to be offered in education departments with a strong RAE research profile.

Meanwhile we await with interest the final report of the pilot STEM review and the consultation on the next iteration of the RAE (the Research Excellence Framework), and in particular whether or not the HE funding councils can continue to resist government pressure to increase the funding of STEM subject areas at the expense of high-performing non-STEM areas such as education. In the meantime we note with some despair the University of Liverpool's recent announcement (*Times Higher*

Education Supplement 2009, 8) that its Department of Sociology may well share the fate of its sometime School of Education, as the university's perception of its RAE 2008 rating is so poor that it may well have to be closed.

References

Bassey, M. 2002. RAE 2001: Analysis of education results. *Research Intelligence* 78: 1–8.

Bassey, M., and Constable, H. 1997. Higher education research in education 1992–1996: Reported in HEFC's RAE. *Research Intelligence* 61: 6–8.

Bence, V., and C. Oppenheim. 2005. The evolution of the UK's research assessment exercise: Publications, performance and perceptions. *Journal of Educational Administration and History* 37, no. 2: 137–55. https://dspace.lboro.ac.uk/dspace-jspui/bitstream/2134/1804/1/benceevolution.pdf (accessed April 9, 2009).

Brown, M. 2009. Outcomes of RAE 2008: UoA 45: Education. Presentation to UCET Research Committee, February 5, Institute of Education, London.

Dadds, M., and Kynch, C. 2003. The impact of RAE 3B rating on educational research in teacher education departments. *Research Intelligence* 84: 8–11.

Department for Education and Skills. 2003. The future of higher education. http://www.dcsf.gov.uk/hegateway/strategy/hestrategy/ (accessed April 9, 2009).

Economic and Social Research Council. 2006. *Demographic review of the UK social sciences.* Swindon, UK: ESRC.

Evidence. 2006. The evaluation of UK research assessment. http://www.tec.govt.nz/upload/downloads/pbrf-report-on-research-evaluation.pdf (accessed April 7, 2009).

Furlong, J. 2004. From the President. *Research Intelligence* 88: 1–2.

Guardian. 2008. Ranking for UK universities in the research assessment exercise 2008. December 18.

Hammersley, M. 1997. Educational research and teaching: A response to David Hargreaves' TTA lecture. *British Educational Research Journal* 23, no. 2: 141–61.

Hargreaves, D. 1996a. *Teaching as a research-based profession: Possibilities and prospects. teacher training agency annual lecture 1996.* London: TTA.

Hargreaves, D. 1996b. Educational research and evidence-based educational practice: A response to critics. *Research Intelligence* 58: 12–16.

Hargreaves, D. 1997. In defence of research for evidence-based teaching: A rejoinder to Martyn Hammersley. *British Educational Research Journal* 23, no. 4: 405–19.

HEFCE. 1997. The impact of the 1992 Research Assessment Exercise on higher education institutions in England. http://www.hefce.ac.uk/pubs/hefce/1997/m6_97.htm (accessed March 20, 2009).

HEFCE. 1999. *Guidance on submissions.* RAE 02/1999. Bristol, UK: HEFCE.

HEFCE. 2000. *Review of research.* Report 00/37. Bristol, UK: HEFCE. http://www.hefce.ac.uk/pubs/hefce/2000/00_37.htm (accessed April 9, 2009).

HEFCE. 2003a. *Review of research assessment.* Bristol, UK: HEFCE. http://www.ra-review.ac.uk/reports/roberts.asp (accessed April 8, 2009).

HEFCE. 2003b. *Circular letter 10/2003.* Bristol, UK: HEFCE. http://www.hefce.ac.uk/pubs/circlets/2003/cl10_03.htm (accessed April 9, 2009).

HEFCE. 2004. *Initial decisions by the UK funding bodies.* Bristol, UK: HEFCE. http://www.rae.ac.uk/pubs/2004/01/rae0401.pdf (accessed April 9, 2009).

HEFCE. 2005. *Guidance on submissions.* RAE 03/2005. Bristol, UK: HEFCE,

HEFCE. 2007. *Membership of RAE 2008 Panels.* RAE 03/2007. Bristol, UK: HEFCE.

HEFCE. 2008. About us. HEFCE. http://www.rae.ac.uk/aboutus/history.asp (accessed April 11, 2009).

HEFCE. 2009. *Recurrent grants for 2009–10.* Bristol, UK: HEFCE. http://www.hefce.ac.uk/pubs/hefce/2009/09_08/ (accessed April 9, 2009).

HERO. 2001. Education panel report RAE 2001. http://www.hero.ac.uk/sites/hero/rae/overview/docs/UoA68.doc (accessed March 24, 2009).

HERO. 2008. Sub-panel 45 education subject overview report RAE 2008. http://www.hero.ac.uk/sites/hero/rae/overview/docs/UoA45.doc (accessed March 24, 2009).

Hillage, J., R. Pearson, A. Anderson, and P. Tamkin. 1998. *Excellence in research on schools research.* Report RR74. London: DfEE.

Her Majesty's Treasury. 2006. *Science and innovation investment framework 2004–1014: Next steps.* London: HMT.

Kerr, D., A. Lines, A. MacDonald, and L. Andrews. 1998. *Mapping education research in England: An analysis of the 1996 Research Assessment Exercise.* Bristol, UK: HEFCE. http://www.hefce.ac.uk/pubs/hefce/1998/98_25.htm (accessed March 20, 2009).

Lawn, M., and J. Furlong. 2007. The social organisation of educational research in England. *European Educational Research Journal* 6, no. 1: 55–70.

Mills, D., A. Jepson, T. Coxon, M. Easterby-Smith, P. Hawkins, and J. Spencer. 2005. *Demographic review of the social sciences. Report to the Economic and Social Research Council.* Swindon, UK: ESRC.

Newall, D. 2003. Scottish higher education policy and funding. In *Scottish education.* 2nd ed., ed. T.G.K. Bryce, and W.M. Humes, 141–50. Edinburgh: Edinburgh University Press.

Oancea, A. 2004a. Distribution of educational research expertise – findings from the analysis of RAE 2001 submission: Part I. *Research Intelligence,* 87: 3–8.

Oancea, A. 2004b. Distribution of educational research expertise – findings from the analysis of RAE 2001 submission: Part II. *Research Intelligence* 88: 3–9.

O'Brian, P. 1997. *The yellow admiral.* London: Harper Collins.

Tapper, T. 2007. *The governance of British higher education: The struggle for policy control.* Dordrecht, The Netherlands: Springer.

Times Higher Education Supplement. 2001. RAE league tables 2001. December 14.

Times Higher Education Supplement. 2008. RAE 2008: The results. December 18.

Times Higher Education Supplement. 2009. RAE panel hurt field by labelling it 'weak'. March 26.

Tooley, J., and D. Darby. 1998. *Educational research: A critique.* London: OfSTED.

Research capacity building in teacher education: Scottish collaborative approaches

Donald Christie[a] and Ian Menter[b]

[a]*Department of Childhood and Primary Studies, University of Strathclyde, Glasgow, G13 1PP, UK;* [b]*Department of Curriculum Studies, University of Glasgow, Glasgow, UK*

This paper examines the context for education research, including teacher education research, in Scotland. Concerns about research capacity are shared with other parts of the UK, but the distinctive context for teacher development and engagement in practitioner research create fertile ground for developments in teacher education research. Schemes such as 'Research to support Schools of Ambition' provide evidence of a shared commitment to teacher research. The national project, 'Applied Education Research Scheme', funded by the Scottish government and the Scottish Funding Council, included a thematic network on learners, learning and teaching. Drawing on activities of this sort, the paper suggests that a key element of effective capacity building lies in collaborative approaches.

Background

For over a decade in the UK and in many other parts of the world it has been acknowledged that there is an urgent need to build research capacity in education in general and in teacher education in particular (Schuller 2007; Munn 2008). During the mid-1990s, several trenchant critiques were launched against the quality of educational research in the UK (Tooley and Darby 1998). The principal criticisms were summarised by Whitty (2006, 161), as follows:

- Lack of rigour
- Failure to produce cumulative findings
- Theoretical incoherence
- Ideological bias
- Irrelevance to schools
- Lack of involvement of teachers
- Inaccessibility and poor dissemination
- Poor cost effectiveness

One response by the university funding bodies and the relevant UK research council, the Economic and Social Research Council (ESRC), to these perceived shortcomings was to establish the Teaching and Learning Research Programme (TLRP) funded through and managed by ESRC beginning in 2000 and expected to run until 2012. This was by far the largest ever such investment in educational research, supporting over 700 educational researchers in some 70 project teams and almost 20 initiatives of cross programme thematic analysis across the four countries of the UK with a total budget at the time of writing of over £43 million. In the Scottish context, the Scottish Higher Education Funding Council and the Scottish Executive Education Department announced their own scheme designed to address perceived weakness in the Scottish universities' performance in research in education as assessed by the UK Research Assessment Exercise (RAE) in 2001, since no higher education institution in Scotland received a top rating at the level of 5 or 5* in 2001 for research in education. The Applied Educational Research Scheme (AERS) was awarded £2 million over a five-year period from 2004 to 2009 and had two principal aims: to build research capacity in education in Scotland; and to use that capacity to carry out worthwhile research directed towards the national priorities for education in Scotland, as described by Munn et al. (2004).

Whitty (2006) has drawn the distinction between two terms used to describe research in education by referring to 'education*al* research' as research concerned in one way or another with improving policy and practice while the term 'education research' should be used more broadly to characterise the whole field. The present article, in considering research capacity building in relation to teacher education, will address both education research and educational research, in the sense that teacher education has to embrace research that addresses broad and fundamental issues to do with learning and pedagogy as well as both research aimed at improving the practice of teacher education and research addressing key aspects of the policy agenda for teacher education. To help with the distinction of different forms and purposes of research in education, Marilyn Cochran-Smith has identified four metaphors for research in the context of teacher education, namely: (a) research as weapon; (b) research as warranty; (c) research as foundation; and (d) research as stance (Cochran-Smith 2007; Cochran-Smith and Lytle 2009).

Research as weapon

This metaphor recognises that research evidence can be used to mount robust challenges to current policy and practice and that research activity itself can have an adversarial, competitive dimension as part of the culture of performativity that has come to govern academic life.

Research as warranty

This metaphor depicts research as providing the warrant or justification for educational proposals and decisions. It highlights the responsibility that rests upon researchers to ensure that the conclusions they reach in reporting the findings of their research are warranted by the evidence they have gathered and the logical coherence of their reasoning. Thus, teacher educators should be researching and generating evidence, which can justify their own pedagogical practices.

Research as foundation

Research can also be seen as the means by which we generate new knowledge; it can provide the foundation on which we build our understanding of the world. This helps us to recognise that research in teacher education should address fundamental questions, e.g. about the nature of learning and about pedagogy which transcend the exigencies of the current political and policy priorities. It is worth noting that the Organisation for Economic Cooperation and Development (OECD) (2002) in its examiners' report on educational research and development in England called for more research in Pasteur's Quadrant, namely, research that *both* enhances our fundamental understanding of (educational) phenomena and at the same time informs practice.

Research as stance

Cochran-Smith (2007) argues that research should be seen as a stance that could usefully be adopted by all who have a legitimate interest in an applied field like teacher education. Teacher educators should be research-minded, adopting a questioning, enquiring approach to their various roles. Cochran-Smith (2003, 8) in describing the role of research, or 'inquiry', in the teaching profession uses the metaphor of stance to suggest:

> …both orientational and positional ideas, to carry allusions to the physical placing of the body as well as to intellectual activities and perspectives over time. In this sense, the metaphor is intended to capture the ways we stand, the ways we see, and the lenses we see through. Teaching is a complex activity that occurs within webs of social, historical, cultural and political significance. Across the life span an inquiry stance provides a kind of grounding within the changing cultures of school reform and competing political agendas.

In this respect, capacity building in teacher education should enable teacher educators to create a culture of evidence that can enhance professional practice in teacher education and hence contribute to enhanced professionalism of teachers, but such a culture should also be characterised by a critical activism (Sachs 2003). By research capacity building we mean attempts to enhance individual and collective research expertise and hence capacities to contribute to improving the quality and quantity of educational research. By collaborative approaches to capacity building we principally have in mind the 'social practices' model, which can be explained as the 'explicit attempt to embed processes for the development of research expertise within the social practices of educational researchers' (Pollard 2007, 643–4). These can be contrasted with individualised approaches such as training courses that introduce research skills in a decontextualised way.

The present article aims first to examine the contextual conditions within which research capacity building in the teacher education sector has taken place during the past 10 years and, second, to evaluate critically the extent to which the distinctively collaborative approaches to research capacity building adopted in Scotland have met the criticisms of educational research identified above. In the following sections we examine the nature and scale of the challenge of research capacity building in Scottish education in general and in Scottish teacher education in particular before considering the distinctively collaborative approaches adopted in order to build research capacity in Scottish teacher education.

Challenge of research capacity building in education and in particular for institutions involved in teacher education

'There is urgency in the need to extend and enhance research capacity that is recognised by the research community, the Scottish Government and the funding council'

(Brown 2008, 39). So wrote Sally Brown in her 'stimulus paper' on Scotland, for the first meeting of the UK Strategic Research Forum for Research in Education, held in 2008.

The great bulk of educational research activity in Scotland takes place in the seven universities that have a school or faculty of education. In each of these seven institutions, teacher education is a core activity that takes place alongside whatever research activity is undertaken. The seven institutional histories differ significantly although there are also some common patterns (Menter 2008). Of the seven, six are 'old' universities, i.e. they existed as universities prior to 1992, and one is a 'new' university (the West of Scotland, formerly Paisley), created in the wake of the 1992 'unification' of higher education. Two universities (Edinburgh and Glasgow) are members of the Russell Group and Universitas 21, respectively UK and international groupings of 'research-led' institutions. Six of the seven faculties are the result of mergers with former colleges of education, the exception being the University of Stirling which created its own Department, later Institute, of Education, when it was established in 1967. Some of the faculties also have provision in related areas such as social work (Strathclyde and Dundee), adult and/or community education (Glasgow, Strathclyde and Dundee) or sports science (Strathclyde and Edinburgh).

The balance of activity within each faculty between teaching and research varies widely and relates both to the institutional histories and to current institutional priorities and strategies. To a large extent there is a 'dual economy' within each faculty, where some staff are primarily teacher educators and others are primarily researchers and, in many cases, there are staff who find themselves experiencing some tension between these two forms of activity. Each institution addresses this tension in different ways, for example by seconding staff from schools or local authorities (sometimes called 'teacher fellows') to carry out significant parts of the teacher education work, thus 'releasing' established staff to undertake more research. Others have different categories of established staff, e.g. 'university lecturers' who are required to undertake research activity, and 'university teachers' who are not.

There have been serious attempts in the institutions to bring about a significant amount of cultural change, in order to ensure that there is at least a reasonable level of high-quality research activity in each case. Given that many of the staff who find themselves working in these faculties were appointed to the antecedent colleges of education, not on the basis of their research expertise and experience, but rather on the basis of successful teaching experience in schools, it is perhaps not surprising that there is evidence of some sense of alienation among significant numbers of staff in some of the institutions. A study of Scottish (and English) teacher education, carried out in 2003–2004 (Menter et al. 2006, 22), reported that:

> staff… highlighted the particular pressures of meeting university expectations at the same time as carrying out other student-focused and partnership activities: 'You get no acknowledgement for the hours you spend organising and trying to get students or tutors to do things, whereas if you write a research paper there is kudos in that' [quotation from tutor].

There can thus be a significant cultural divide within the faculties of education – between teaching and research – and the managers in these faculties have been attempting to ensure that the negative effects of this divide are minimised, indeed that teaching and research are brought into a synergistic relationship where possible (as indicated in Menter, Brisard and Smith 2006; see also Munn and Baron 2008).

Table 1. Total research excellence funding for education in Scottish universities by the Scottish Funding Council.

2001–2002 (funding prior to RAE 2001 results)	2008–2009 (funding prior to the RAE 2008 results)	2009–2010 (first round of funding after RAE 2008)
£2,841,687	£3,005,875	£3,763,172

The majority of the seven universities made a return in education to the 2001 RAE (Aberdeen and Paisley did not), and four submissions were awarded a Grade 4 (Edinburgh, Glasgow, Stirling [which alone had achieved a Grade 5 in 1996] and Strathclyde) and therefore received a reasonable level of research funding from the funding council. Dundee made a small return in 2001 and gained a Grade 3a and thus received small-scale funding (in England Grade 3s were not awarded any funding) (Kirkwood 2002).

In 2008, all seven universities with an education faculty, and also Glasgow Caledonian University, which has a unit specialising in community and adult education, made returns to the RAE in education, making a total of eight submissions from Scotland. On the new rating system, seven of the eight – the seven faculties of education – were judged to have some activity at the very highest 'world-leading' level. A total of 258 active researchers were returned, compared with 163 in 2001, which represents a very significant 58% expansion of the volume of educational research activity in Scotland – against the trend in the rest of the UK. Although there was an increase in the volume of each submission in most cases, one of the high achievers in 2001 (Stirling) actually saw a decline in volume in 2008, although it achieved the highest Grade Profile Average in Scotland (2.60). If we put some of these achievements in the wider UK context, it is interesting to note that three of the five largest submissions across the four jurisdictions are from Scotland (Edinburgh, Glasgow and Strathclyde), alongside the Institute of Education, University of London and the Open University.

In the wake of the 2008 RAE, research funding will now come to all seven faculties of education in Scotland, with the majority of faculties, although not all, receiving an increased sum compared with the 2001–2008 period. The total sums allocated by the Funding Council in relation to education research are shown in Table 1.

The figures in Table 1 show a 32% increase in funding from 2001 to 2009/10, significantly less than the proportionate increase in the numbers of researchers.

The context for teacher education in Scotland

Having examined the university context for education research, including teacher education research, we turn now to consider the wider professional and policy context in Scotland. The internal cultures of faculties of education and their university settings are only one part of the wider picture that is significant in the discussion of research capacity. These faculties are also necessarily interacting with the wider professional and political community of education and teacher education and are required to be responsive to policy developments instigated externally.

Pre-devolution studies of the education policy community in Scotland stressed the close relationships between the various stakeholders and the inherent conservatism that sometimes appeared to ensue from this. It might have been anticipated that the removal of formal responsibility for education from the UK's New Labour government in London to the Scottish Executive in Edinburgh might have unsettled such 'cosiness' and also that the influence of New Labour approaches may be less prevalent in Scotland than in England. The processes of change in Scotland appear to have been less radical and introduced at a slower pace than in England; however, they have been achieved through a more consensual process and so in the long term are likely to be more embedded than those in England.

A scoping study carried out for the TLRP revealed that the ways in which teaching (and learning) is defined through formal policy statements in Scotland does differ from elsewhere in the UK. In particular, there is greater emphasis on teaching as an intellectual and theoretically informed occupation, with a strong sense of social purpose and of professional activity being based on clearly stated values (Hulme and Menter 2008).

This emphasis appears to relate to the (usually) strongly consensual nature of the policy community in Scotland in which a wide range of stakeholders, including a long-established General Teaching Council, have significant voices in the processes. The recent 'modernisation' of teaching took a significantly distinctive form in Scotland (by comparison with the rest of the UK), with much more emphasis on development than on performativity and assessment (Menter, Mahony and Hextall 2004). Humes (2007) points out, however, that consensus may not necessarily be a good basis for independent and critical research activity.

Although responsibility for education and training was formally devolved from the UK Government and Westminster Parliament to the Scottish Parliament and the Scottish Executive in July 1999, Scotland's education system has long enjoyed relative autonomy from England. It is often argued that education occupies a special place in Scottish history and culture. The administrative (but not the political) autonomy of Scotland's educational framework was guaranteed in the Act of Union of 1707. Education, along with the law and the Church, continues to be regarded as one of the key institutions in Scottish social and cultural life (Humes and Bryce 2003). The powerful shaping 'myth' that informs education policy in (an increasingly diverse) Scotland is summarised as follows:

> Scottish society is relatively egalitarian and meritocratic; that ability and achievement, not rank, should determine success in the world; that public (rather than private) institutions should be the means of trying to bring about the good society; and that, even where merit does justify differential rewards, there are certain basic respects – arising from the common humanity of men and women – in which human beings deserve equal consideration and treatment. (Humes and Bryce 2003, 109)

The professional status of teachers is more rigorously protected and the power of teachers' professional associations/trade unions is stronger within the Scottish policy network. Scotland's professional body for teachers, the General Teaching Council was established in 1966, some 35 years ahead of the other three countries which make up the UK (McIver 2008), and the vast majority of teachers are represented by a single teachers' union – the Educational Institute of Scotland (EIS), founded in 1847 and awarded a Royal Charter in 1851 (Forrester 2008). Prior to political devolution, Scotland resisted the move to standardised tests implemented in England and Wales and developed national guidelines for its own broadly based *5–14 Curriculum* through processes of consultation and gradual implementation; processes that continue to support the current development of a revised curriculum, *A Curriculum for Excellence*

(Scottish Executive 2004). A stable policy community has mediated external influences on policy and commentators have suggested that the dissonance between the profession and central government evident in England is not a feature of policy-making in Scotland. Nixon et al. (2006, 279) suggest that Scotland was able to resist the powerful centralising tendencies experienced in England and Wales because 'the deep "codes" of teacher professionalism north of the border reinforce many of the priorities and myths of central government'.

The report of the McCrone Inquiry into the conditions of service and pay for teachers in Scotland was published in May 2000. A tripartite Implementation Group representing teachers' organisations, employers (through the Convention of Scottish Local Authorities) and the Scottish Executive was established the following September. This approach was in line with the generally consultative style referred to previously. An agreement was reached in January 2001 with the publication of *A teaching profession for the twenty first century* (Scottish Executive 2001). The introduction to this document makes reference to a '...unique process of discussion and dialogue', which signposts a new way of working:

> We have agreed that, for the future, the working relationships between teacher organisations, employers and the Scottish Executive will be based on mutual respect and understanding, on shared responsibility and on the shared development of ideas and programmes for change. (Scottish Executive 2001, 1)

McCrone also sought to address the 'hierarchical nature of teacher culture in Scotland' (MacDonald 2004, 414) by simplifying and flattening the career structure to afford greater opportunities for non-promoted teachers. This has seen a reduction in promoted (middle management) posts in secondary schools. The grade or status (rather than 'post') of Chartered Teacher (CT) was introduced to provide the opportunity for salary increments without management responsibilities for those teachers who choose to 'stay within the classroom' (O'Brien and Hunt 2005; Kirk, Smith and Beveridge 2003; Connolly and McMahon 2007). The Chartered Teacher Programme was introduced in August 2003 and is open to all teachers who have reached the top of the main grade teachers' pay scale and who have maintained a continuing professional development (CPD) portfolio.

There is no doubt that the concepts of research and enquiry have entered the discourse of teacher professionalism in Scotland. As part of the new framework of professional standards for teachers in Scotland, for example, the Standard for Chartered Teacher (SCT) seeks to describe the knowledge, attributes, values and professional action associated with accomplished teaching and which are to be expected of those aspiring to the status of CT (Scottish Executive 2002). The significance of research for the teaching profession is signalled within the SCT, in the clear expectation that the CT should demonstrate the capacity to:

> ...ensure that teaching is informed by reading and research. For example, by:
>
> - engaging in professional enquiry and action research, and applying findings
> - reflecting critically on research evidence and modifying practice as appropriate
> - testing whether a particular theoretical perspective actually applies in practice
> - interpreting changes to education policy and practice and
> - contributing and responding to such changes
>
> (Scottish Executive 2002)

Kirk (2004) has argued that teachers have tended in the past to be the 'objects or consumers' of research rather than its generators and goes on to claim that the text of the SCT calls for teachers to take a much more active role in initiating and engaging in research activities and rigorous critical analysis, as integral components of their professional practice, as well as applying research evidence generated by others to their own context. The implications of the CT programme are considered further later.

A commitment to the development of teachers as autonomous professionals can also be identified in a number of policies, such as: the formative assessment programme, Assessment is for Learning; the new school curriculum, *Curriculum for Excellence* (see later); and indeed the AERS itself. But one of the policies that is most explicitly based on a commitment to teacher development is the relatively new school improvement scheme, Schools of Ambition. Working with teachers in 52 secondary schools across Scotland, each of which has devised its own 'Transformational Plan', a team of university-based researchers is supporting the evaluation by school staff of the implementation of the plan, through the development of various models of action research (Hulme, Lowden and Elliot 2009). This work had revealed a range of influences on teachers' professional identity and development as well as on the development of schools as 'learning organisations' and/or as 'communities of enquiry' (Cassidy et al. 2008). Research-oriented approaches to school development were found to cover a spectrum from the 'instrumental' to the 'developmental', sometimes reflecting the level of confidence among the teachers involved and sometimes reflecting the organisational culture of the school. Nevertheless the range of experiences includes examples where an enquiry orientation is likely to be sustained (Menter and Hulme forthcoming).

The preceding brief review suggests that the formation of teacher education policy in Scotland may be more consultative and premised on higher degrees of trust than may be found elsewhere in the UK. Much policy development is founded on the priorities that emerged from the National Debate on Education held in 2002 (Munn et al. 2004). But in the context of the discussion here the first key point is that the incorporation of a research and enquiry element in teaching and teacher education is well established, at least in terms of formal policy. Second, the commitment to research is very much a commitment to *applied* educational research, including forms of teacher/practitioner research.

Collaborative approaches to research capacity building

From its inception, the AERS was a funding scheme for applied educational research that was distinctively Scottish, displaying several of the general characteristics described previously. In particular, at the meeting called in 2002 to launch the scheme and invite bids from interested parties, the clear message was conveyed that collaboration was to be encouraged. Three forms of collaboration were presaged: first, collaboration between educational researchers and academics from other social science disciplines; second, collaboration among researchers across the various higher education institutions with an interest in education as a discipline or a field of enquiry, including, of course, the seven teacher education institutions in Scotland; and third, collaboration between educational researchers and other stakeholders in education, namely, teachers and other professional practitioners, policy makers and local politicians.

Colleagues from the four faculties or departments of education which had received RAE ratings of '4' in RAE 2001, Edinburgh, Strathclyde, Stirling and Glasgow formed a group to prepare a comprehensive bid for the whole sum available, £2 million, rather than compete for smaller amounts. In the event the proposal was led by a consortium comprising the Universities of Edinburgh, Stirling and Strathclyde, Glasgow having chosen to pursue an independent bid. The collaborative bid was to create four collaborative research networks, three networks to conduct projects addressing substantive research themes and one network to lead the research capacity building efforts of the scheme. The thematic networks were the Learners, Learning and Teaching Network, the School Management and Governance Network and the Schools and Social Capital Network, each undertaking three substantive projects over the five-year funding period 2004–2009. There were opportunities to participate in each of these research networks at three different levels as shown in Figure 1.

Level 1: 'Entry level'

Interested 'users', observers, or potential participants who wish to be kept informed of developments in a network and of network events, which they might wish to attend.

- *'Membership' at this level means being included in the mailing list for electronic and other forms of communications in order to receive information from the network;*
- *This level of membership also means being able to communicate with the network to express views, make suggestions, contribute and exchange ideas as part of ongoing discussions.*
- *This level of membership is open and 'free'*

Level 2: 'Active membership'

Researchers and other stakeholders who are taking an active role in some aspect of the activities of a network, such as:

- *Membership of the Network Coordinating Group,*
- *Direct involvement in research activity associated with the planned projects of the network, for example, participating in a recognised community of enquiry related to the themes being explored by the network.*
- *Active membership would require an authorised commitment being made to give time to the activity associated with participation in the network.*

Level 3: Close involvement ('Core membership')

Close involvement in the work of a network would apply to a relatively small number of individuals at any one time. We are referring here to the membership of the project teams established for each of the planned projects and any others who are closely connected with the projects either through some form of mentoring arrangement or more formal 'apprenticeship'.

- *This form of membership will require a substantial, institutionally authorised commitment on the part of participants in terms of time and effort.*
- *Benefits of participation would include opportunities to co-author papers, 'hands on' experience of data collection and analysis, possibilities of co-authoring research grant applications, and developing project management skills.*

Figure 1. Levels of participation in the Applied Educational Research Scheme networks. Note: two-way arrows signify that movement between levels in either direction may be expected over time.

Participants in AERS were drawn from across the country and from a range of different professional backgrounds. However, participation from the research and practitioner communities was not evenly spread across the three levels. For example, few teachers were able to give the kind of commitment required for participation at levels two or three. To address this, strategies such as identifying sources of funding to allow teachers to be released from class-time duties so that they could participate fully at levels two and three, as shown in Figure 1, were developed to promote opportunities for a small number of practitioners to join project teams that predominantly comprised university researchers. Conversely, AERS forged links with existing policy-related educational initiatives in the field and school-based development work, in order to enable university academic researchers to engage with existing groups composed of professional practitioners.

An inclusive, collaborative, approach to research capacity building, described by Baron (2005, 15) as an embedded 'social practices model' was adopted by the AERS networks (Rees et al. 2007; Munn 2008). Offering opportunities for active participation in all stages of the research process was seen as the key to building capacity. Thus, inexperienced researchers were encouraged to join with more experienced colleagues in teams formed within each of the three networks to carry out the research projects, which were only schematically planned within the original proposal. This was to allow participants to contribute to the precise formulation of research questions as well as all other phases of the projects through reviewing relevant literature, designing research instruments, data collection, data analysis and the range of reporting, publication and dissemination activities. Participants in the work of the networks represented a wide range of stakeholder groups. As well as researchers from all seven of the university teacher education institutions, teachers and other professional practitioners, education managers and policy makers at local and national levels and representatives of other relevant bodies came together to engage in the research. Munn (2008, 426) described this form of collaboration as a 'new approach to knowledge production involving a range of stakeholders'.

As part of this social practices approach, the AERS Fellowships scheme was initiated. This provided a means by which emerging researchers seeking to become part of the community of practice of educational research could make a more formal commitment to the work of the relevant network project and have mentoring arrangements formalised and tailored to their particular needs through a fellowship agreement which was regularly reviewed by all parties, including a representative of the Fellow's 'home' institution or organisation. This part of AERS proved very successful with a total of 22 inexperienced researchers appointed as AERS Fellows across the four networks. These were predominantly early career academic staff in the university sector, but included several local authority employees and colleagues from other stakeholder agencies. Through the scheme they rapidly gained experience of research management as well as other research processes, equipping them to take on the role of principal investigator in other studies, in some cases leading bids for external research funding.

The fourth AERS network, the Research Capacity Building Network, was responsible for more formal and technical aspects of research training through the creation and delivery of a suite of modules designed for online access and through organising training events in response to specific needs identified by the other networks. The modular materials formed the core of the master's in Applied Educational Research at the University of Strathclyde which subsequently received ESRC recognition for post-graduate research training in education. The modular materials themselves comprise around 70 resource units, 55 of which are to be made available, along with units created by TLRP, through the British Educational Research Association (BERA) website under a Creative Commons form of copyright, with responsibility for their long-term maintenance and development passing to BERA. The idea is that these unit materials can in future be accessed and combined flexibly by individuals and institutions according to needs and preferences.

In the Learners, Learning and Teaching Network, Project 1 (LLT1) was designed to explore and develop the concept of the Community of Enquiry as a collaborative model for research in education. Drawing on literature related to practical philosophical inquiry, communities of practice and activity theory, the project team argued that such an approach could enhance the ecological validity of research in educational contexts and identified seven key factors or considerations for putative communities of enquiry (Cassidy et al. 2008, 217). These were:

- A community depends on its members' opportunities to engage in dialogue and other modes of participation.
- Participation in a community is sustained through the quality of relationships.
- Perspectives and assumptions underpin the relationships of a community and may offer insights into the dynamics and operation of the community.
- How a community operates is governed by its structure and context, including the extent to which its structure is imposed or constrained either internally or externally.
- As a community develops, a climate for its operation also emerges – involving aspects such as tone, environment and potential conflict.
- The purpose of an enquiry will influence this climate and there may be a need to accommodate or harmonise a multiplicity of purposes arising from the complex interrelationships, perspectives and assumptions involved.
- A key issue for all communities is control, in relation to who has access to the community, to resources, constraints and power within it.

By dint of their collaborative nature, it could be argued that communities of enquiry have a strong potential to build research capacity among participants if such factors as those listed above are taken into account.

An important feature of the communities of enquiry that were the focus of the investigation of LLT1 was the use of the Virtual Research Environment (VRE) as a tool to support collaborative research activity. The VRE provided a range of collaborative research tools such as discussion space, a shared file store, shared writing tools, schedules, announcements, email alerts and archives. It had been the original intention of the project to support and track the progress of a small number of groups aspiring to become collaborative communities of enquiry. In the event, such was the interest in the use of the VRE that a very large number of such groups sought and were provided with VRE workspaces (at the time of writing, the number of groups using the VRE exceeds 170). These include multidisciplinary groups established to explore issues such as disability and communities of enquiry in which school pupils have been co-enquirers with teachers and researchers involved in developing new curricular approaches in areas such as education for citizenship, as well as collaborative research teams with geographically and institutionally distributed membership. The VRE has also been adopted in other funded research such as the Research to Support the Schools of Ambition, mentioned earlier, in which it provided the means for shared communication and the pooling of resources among participating schools and the potential tools for collaborative activity.

The current policy context for teacher education in Scotland is heavily influenced by the reform of the curriculum for children and young people aged 3–18, *Curriculum for Excellence* (Scottish Executive 2004). This can be seen as providing opportunities for teacher educators and along with other educational researchers to engage collaboratively with teachers, pupils and other stakeholders including student teachers in transformational research activities focusing on the development and implementation of the new curriculum outcomes and experiences. Discussions have taken place between the AERS LLT Network, colleagues in the Scottish curriculum body, Learning and Teaching Scotland, and the team responsible for introducing 'GLOW', the digital network which is to connect all schools and provide every pupil and every teacher in every Scottish school with powerful networking, information and communications tools. There are very interesting possibilities for collaborative research and enquiry to enhance the evidence base informing the ongoing process of curriculum reform in inclusive and interesting ways and at the same time offer further opportunities for research capacity building in education, especially as teacher educators in Scotland are working towards a framework of standards in which research and enquiry skills and dispositions are seen as vital elements of teacher professionalism (Christie 2008).

The importance of collaborative approaches to teachers' professional development and the potential of collaborative forms of capacity building activity have been highlighted by the work of the LLT Network project on 'Teachers as Learners', which has developed a 'Triple-Lens Framework' in order to make sense of the multiple factors influencing teachers' professional learning (Fraser et al. 2007). Evidence from several series of interviews with teachers, education managers and other key informants and from an online survey of teachers showed that teachers strongly value informal support from, and professional dialogue with colleagues and that they value opportunities to work collaboratively in small groups on issues firmly located in their own school context (Christie, Fraser, et al. 2009). While there was evidence of a strong aspiration towards collaborative forms of professional learning and CPD, in practice, there are structural features within the system; in particular, individualised forms of accountability, which appear to militate against collaboration. Thus, where schools are attempting to operate as learning communities, there is evidence that 'social and informal dimensions of professional development are increasingly valued, but this can create tensions with what is recognised and perceived as accountable within the system' (Christie, Fraser, et al. 2009, 1).

Other major pieces of funded research in Scotland also point towards the significance of social, relational aspects of teachers' professional learning and thus are relevant to the present discussion of capacity building in teacher education. For example, McNally et al. (2008), who led the Early Professional Learning project, funded by TLRP, using innovative methodologies including the recruitment of teacher researchers to the project team, showed that the informal, emotional–relational dimension was of the highest importance for newly qualified teachers in their personal journeys towards full registration through the induction year.

The process of collaboration was itself investigated by another TLRP-funded project which focused on collaborative group work in Scottish primary schools

(Christie, Thurston, et al. 2009). The quality of collaborative dialogue taking place during group work was found to be a strong predictor of the significant learning gains achieved in the primary classrooms (Howe et al. 2007). However, engagement in constructive collaboration cannot be taken for granted. It requires effort and commitment and the acquisition of the social and communication skills, essential prerequisites for effective group working.

If we consider research to be about creating new knowledge, the parallels become clear between the processes of research and professional enquiry on the one hand, and fundamental processes of learning on the other. Collaborative research, just as collaborative learning, entails, *inter alia*:

- engagement in constructive dialogue;
- shared commitment to shared purposes aimed in some way towards action;
- sharing (in the sense of exchanging) perspectives and assumptions;
- mutual respect and trust;
- effective planning, organisation and management.

However, collaboration is not a panacea for either classroom learning or research and research capacity building. In the classroom context, collaborative approaches are more appropriate for certain kinds of learning objectives, particularly where new enhanced understandings are sought, but are less so where the acquisition or practice of individual skills is required (Damon and Phelps 1989). Similarly in relation to research capacity building, the collaborative social practices model was deemed to have been an essential component of the AERS in Scotland (AERS 2009), but it was not the whole story. The capacity building strategy also involved the development of on-line training resources which provided for individual skills training in research methodology, as required. Fitness for purpose must be the key consideration in any decisions about the selection of strategy and approaches both in pedagogy and in research capacity building.

Thus it can be argued that, over the five-year period from 2004 to 2009, the conditions were created in which the level of engagement in research could be enhanced among teacher educators in Scotland through new opportunities to collaborate in substantive research activity. Teacher educators who had previously been inexperienced researchers gained experience of all aspects of the research process. In this way, individual research capacity was enhanced. The collaborative involvement of other stakeholders in the research activities of the AERS projects not only enabled these stakeholders to gain research experience themselves, but also contributed to building collective research capacity by enhancing the quality of the research being carried out in terms of its relevance and ecological validity (AERS 2009). The significant increase (reported previously) in the numbers of education academics, including teacher educators, recognised by the national RAE in 2008 as being research active and producing work of national and international importance can be taken as a measure of increased research capacity within the field of education in Scotland.

If we consider this alongside the changes in the educational research landscape created by the AERS, it can be inferred that the collaborative approaches which were an intrinsic part of the scheme have contributed to obviating at least some of the shortcomings of educational research summarised by Whitty (2006, 161). In particular, the issues of 'irrelevance to schools' and 'lack of involvement of teachers' were quite explicitly addressed by defining the purposes of the research projects in relation to national priorities for education and by offering new opportunities for practitioners to collaborate in research with academic researchers and policy makers.

Turning to 'lack of rigour' and 'theoretical incoherence', the AERS (2009) final report claims a total of 25 articles directly attributable to the research activities of the collaborative projects conducted by the AERS networks having been published by December 2008 in peer-reviewed journals, whose responsibility it is to maintain standards of theoretical and methodological rigour and coherence. In relation to 'poor cost effectiveness', the potential value of collaborative engagement as perceived by education faculty managers prompted significant investment in terms of staff time and resources, which was estimated to have more than doubled the original funding provided (AERS 2009). This investment could be argued to have been very cost effective in terms of fostering research activity in that it yielded no fewer than a total of 707 'registrations' for involvement in the research of the AERS networks across the three levels of participation indicated in Figure 1 (AERS 2009). In terms of research capability, the effectiveness of the AERS Research Fellowship scheme is indicated by the successes of the 20 AERS Fellows who had learning contracts and who, for example, have not only achieved peer-reviewed publications, but have also subsequently progressed to become principal investigators in their own funded projects.

Conclusions

The Scottish context affords a number of unique opportunities and advantages for teacher education. Nevertheless, teacher educators in Scotland face similar challenges as have been identified elsewhere, for example, through the ESRC demographic review of research capacity (Mills et al. 2006) and through the pervasive culture of performativity which increasingly infuses public services across the globe and not only in the OECD countries which have collectively been struck by shockwaves of turbulence in their financial systems. Collaborative approaches to research in general and to research capacity building in particular, while not a panacea, may be effective in the kinds of conditions which currently prevail across the UK.

First, there are good theoretical and ethical justifications for adopting a more collaborative approach. Research is a social practice with its own cultural tools and specialised language and proficiency with these comes through active engagement in research activity. Collaborative approaches also lend themselves to building both cultural and social capital (Baron, Field and Schuller 2000). Collaborative approaches are intrinsically participative and thus have the potential to be more inclusive.

Second, there are good methodological justifications for collaborative approaches. Given that education is an applied and practice-based field of enquiry, collaborative approaches to research are arguably more ecologically valid, especially where research teams include the professional practitioners who actually mediate the learning processes. Furthermore collaborative approaches are arguably both economically and political sound. Collaborative approaches offer the potential for pooling scarce resources in terms of methodological knowledge and skill and they articulate well with a wide range of political policy imperatives which call for 'joined-up' thinking and inter-professional practice.

The collaborative, social practices model of research capacity building, distinctively developed over recent years in Scotland by AERS, has already proved to be highly influential across the wider national and international arenas. First, it provided the basis of the UK ESRC's TLRP Phase 2 Capacity Building strategy. Second, it was the impetus behind the funding of the two phases of the Welsh Educational Research Network (see the article by Tanner and Davies in this issue) and the funding by ESRC of two pilot regional capacity building networks, including the Teacher Education Research Network based in the Northwest of England. Third, it was the subject of Munn's Presidential Address to BERA in 2007 and of the BERA Address to the Australian Educational Research Association Conference where uptake of the model is being considered. Finally, the AERS Fellowship model was directly replicated in TLRP's 'Meeting of Minds' scheme through which 25 early career researchers received mentoring from senior colleagues beyond their own institutions (AERS 2009). The potential advantages of collaborative approaches extending across the UK, Europe and beyond have not yet fully been recognised, far less realised. However, it is interesting that the foundations have already been laid for a World Educational Research Association, in which the SERA and BERA (Scottish and British Educational Research Associations), are actively involved.

For teacher education, therefore, the implications are clear. Teacher educators should be prepared to engage in new forms of collaborative partnerships, involving as appropriate, schools, teachers, pupils, parents, community groups, local authorities and other relevant agencies. Teacher educators will perhaps become more aware of their own needs in terms of research capacity building when they consider fully their responsibility to equip their students to become both collaborative professional enquirers and innovative curriculum developers as explicitly demanded by the standards frameworks for the teaching profession now well established in Scotland and as increasingly being recognised as important elsewhere in the world (Darling-Hammond 2001). In this context, it is interesting that more nuanced collective meanings of professional competence are now being explored internationally (Grangeat and Gray 2008). Furthermore, teacher educators should celebrate the opportunities they enjoy, perhaps uniquely, to bring their research, their teaching and their knowledge exchange portfolios into close, synergistic alignment. Returning to Cochran-Smith's (2007) metaphors for research, the various opportunities for, and approaches to, research capacity building described in the present article should equip and encourage teacher educators to adopt research as an *inquiry stance* and thereby contribute to a culture of evidence in teacher education. Teacher educators, through their engagement in research, can hope both to create a stronger evidential *warrant* for their practices and to build a stronger *foundation* for their understanding of the learning processes inherent in teacher education and professional development.

Acknowledgement

Parts of one section of this article draw upon an earlier paper by Ian Menter and Moira Hulme, 'Policy making in teacher education and professional development in Scotland' presented at the BERA Conference 2008, as part of a symposium convened by Donald Christie, 'Teachers as Learners: Evidence from major funded research in Scotland'. Thanks to Moira Hulme for her contribution.

References

Applied Educational Research Scheme. 2009. *Final report.* Edinburgh, UK: AERS.

Baron, S. 2005. TLRP's phase 2 research capacities building strategy. *BERA Research Intelligence* 93: 14–17.

Baron, S., J. Field, and T. Schuller, eds. 2000. *Social capital: Critical perspectives.* Oxford, UK: Oxford University Press.

Brown, S. 2008. Capacity and quality in education research in Scotland: A stimulus report. SFRE. http://www.sfre.ac.uk/wp-content/uploads/2009/03/scot-report-forum-1.pdf

Cassidy, C., D. Christie, N. Coutts, J. Dunn, C. Sinclair, D. Skinner, and A. Wilson. 2008. Building communities of educational enquiry. *Oxford Review of Education* 34, no. 2: 217–35.

Christie, D. 2008. Benchmarks and standards in teaching. In *Scottish education: Third edition, beyond devolution,* ed. T. Bryce and W. Humes, 845–54. Edinburgh, UK: Edinburgh University Press.

Christie, D., C. Fraser, A. Kennedy, S. McKinney, L. Reid, M. Welsh, A. Wilson, L. Seagraves, and E. Karagiannidou. 2009. *AERS briefing paper 9: Understanding teachers as learners.* Glasgow, UK: AERS/University of Strathclyde.

Christie, D., A. Thurston, A. Tolmie, C. Howe, and K. Topping. 2009. Supporting group work in Scottish primary classrooms: Improving the quality of collaborative dialogue. *Cambridge Journal of Education* 39, no. 1: 135–50.

Cochran-Smith, M. 2003. Learning and unlearning: The education of teacher educators. *Teaching and Teacher Education* 19: 5–28.

Cochran-Smith, M. 2007. Research and evidence in teacher education. Keynote Lecture presented at the Teacher Education and Teachers' Work Conference, June 15, in Glasgow.

Cochran-Smith, M., and S. Lytle. 2009. *Inquiry as stance.* New York: Teachers' College Press.

Connolly, G., and M. McMahon. 2007. Chartered teacher: Accrediting professionalism for Scotland's teachers – a view from the inside. *Journal of In-Service Education* 33, no. 1: 91–105.

Damon, W., and E. Phelps. 1989. Critical distinctions among three approaches to peer education. *International Journal of Educational Research* 58: 9–19.

Darling-Hammond, L. 2001. Standard setting in teaching: Changes is licensing, certification and assessment. In *Handbook of research on teaching.* 4th ed., ed. V. Richardson, 751–76. Washington, DC: American Educational Research Association.

Forrester, F. 2008. Teachers' professional organisations. In *Scottish education.* 3rd ed., *Beyond devolution,* ed. T. Bryce and W. Humes, 881–85. Edinburgh, UK: Edinburgh University Press.

Fraser, C., A. Kennedy, L. Reid, and S. McKinney. 2007. Teachers' continuing professional development (CPD): Contested concepts, understandings and models. *Journal of In-Service Education* 33, no. 2: 153–69.

Grangeat, M., and P. Gray. 2008. Teaching as collective work: Analysis, current research and implications for teacher education. *Journal of Education for Teaching* 34, no. 3: 177–89.

Howe, C., A. Tolmie, A. Thurston, K. Topping, D. Christie, K. Livingston, E. Jessiman, and C. Donaldson. 2007. Group work in elementary science: Organisational principles for classroom teaching. *Learning and Instruction* 17: 549–63.

Hulme, M., K. Lowden, and D. Elliot. 2009. Teachers as researchers: Initial experiences within the Scottish 'Schools of Ambition'. *Teacher Education and Teachers' Work* 1: 18–30.

Hulme, M., and I. Menter. 2008. Learning to teach in post-devolution UK: A technical or an ethical process? *Southern African Review of Education* 14, nos. 1–2: 43–64.

Humes, W. 2007. The infrastructure of educational research in Scotland. *European Educational Research Journal* 6, no. 1: 71–86.

Humes, W., and T. Bryce. 2003. The distinctiveness of Scottish education. In *Scottish education*. 2nd ed., *Post-devolution*, ed. T. Bryce and W. Humes, 98–110. Edinburgh, UK: Edinburgh University Press.

Kirk, G. 2004. The chartered teacher: A challenge to the profession in Scotland. *Education in the North* 11: 10–17.

Kirk, G., I. Smith, and W. Beveridge. 2003. *The chartered teacher*. Edinburgh, UK: Dunedin Press.

Kirkwood, M. 2002. Educational research in Scotland. *Research Intelligence* 79: 33–40.

MacDonald, A. 2004. Collegiate or compliant? Primary teachers in post-McCrone Scotland. *British Educational Research Journal* 30: 413–33.

McIver, M. 2008. The General Teaching Council. In *Scottish education*. 3rd ed., *Beyond devolution*, ed. T. Bryce and W. Humes, 886–93. Edinburgh, UK: Edinburgh University Press.

McNally, J., A. Blake, B. Corbin, and P. Gray. 2008. Finding an identity and meeting a standard: Connecting the conflicting in teacher induction. *Journal of Education Policy* 23, no. 3: 287–98.

Menter, I. 2008. Teacher education institutions. In *Scottish education*. 3rd ed., *Beyond devolution*, ed. T. Bryce and W. Humes, 817–25. Edinburgh, UK: Edinburgh University Press.

Menter, I., E. Brisard, and I. Smith. 2006. *Convergence or divergence? Initial teacher education in Scotland and England*. Edinburgh, UK: Dunedin Academic Press.

Menter, I., and M. Hulme. Forthcoming. Teacher researchers in the UK: What are their needs? Some lessons from Scotland. In *Connecting enquiry and professional learning in education: Joining the dots*, ed. A. Campbell and S. Groundwater-Smith. London: Routledge.

Menter, I., P. Mahony, and I. Hextall. 2004. Ne'er the twain shall meet? The modernisation of the teaching workforce in Scotland and England. *Journal of Education Policy* 19, no. 2: 195–214.

Mills, D., A. Jepson, T. Coxon, M. Easterby-Smith, P. Hawkins, and J. Spencer. 2006. *Demographic review of the social sciences*. Swindon, UK: ESRC.

Munn, P. 2008. Building research capacity collaboratively. *British Educational Research Journal* 34, no. 4: 413–30.

Munn, P., and S. Baron. 2008. Research and practice. In *Scottish education*. 3rd ed., *Beyond devolution*, ed. T. Bryce and W. Humes, 864–72. Edinburgh, UK: Edinburgh University Press.

Munn, P., J. Stead, G. MacLeod, J. Brown, M. Cowie, G. McCluskey, A. Pirrie, and J. Scott. 2004. Schools for the 21st century: The national debate on education in Scotland. *Research Papers in Education* 19, no. 4: 433–52.

Nixon, J., P. Cope, J. McNally, S. Rodrigues, and C. Stephen. 2006. University-based initial teacher education: Institutional re-positioning and professional renewal. In *Teacher education: Major themes in education*. Vol. 5, *Globalisation, standards and teacher education*, ed. D. Hartley and M. Whitehead, 274–92. London: Routledge.

O'Brien, J., and G. Hunt. 2005. A new professionalism? Becoming a chartered teacher – part 1. *Teacher Development* 9: 447–66.

Organisation for Economic Cooperation and Development. 2002. *Educational research and development in England: Examiners' report*. Paris: OECD.

Pollard, A. 2007. The UK's teaching and learning research programme: Findings and significance. *British Educational Research Journal* 33, no. 5: 639–46.

Rees, G., S. Baron, R. Boyask, and C. Taylor. 2007. Research capacity building, professional learning and the social practices of educational research. *British Educational Research Journal* 33, no. 5: 761–79.

Sachs, J. 2003. *The activist teaching profession.* Buckingham, UK: Open University Press.

Schuller, T. 2007. Capacity building in educational research: Sketching an international picture. *Scottish Educational Review* 39, no. 1: 84–91.

Scottish Executive. 2001. *A teaching profession for the 21st century.* Edinburgh, UK: Scottish Executive.

Scottish Executive. 2002. *Chartered teacher.* Edinburgh, UK: Scottish Executive.

Scottish Executive. 2004. *A curriculum for excellence.* Edinburgh, UK: Scottish Executive.

Tooley, J., and D. Darby. 1998. *Educational research – a critique: A survey of published educational research.* London: Office for Standards in Education.

Whitty, G. 2006. Education(al) research and education policy: Is conflict inevitable? *British Educational Research Journal* 32, no. 2: 159–76.

Harnessing the slipstream: building educational research capacity in Northern Ireland. Size matters

Ruth Leitch

School of Education, Queen's University, Belfast, Northern Ireland

Northern Ireland is uniquely distinguished from England, Scotland and Wales, by being a society in transition, emerging from a prolonged period of civil conflict and political instability that has affected its infrastructure and has increased the need for co-ordinated and specialist research. The current paper traces some of the systemic challenges and opportunities for educational research capacity building that arise from Northern Ireland being uniquely positioned as a small polity and critically appraises how initiatives elsewhere to build capacity in teacher education, while providing valuable exemplars, are unlikely to transfer readily to this context. Rather, building on an expanded definition of research capacity, Northern Ireland needs to capitalise cautiously on the current climate of openness between policy-maker and researcher communities. In so doing, the goals are to develop a shared, cohesive agenda, provide a sound evidence base, improve research support and harness the strengths and pockets of excellence that exist. All of these should simultaneously meet local research priorities, address the developmental capacity building needs of local researchers, while at the same time contributing to local, national and international knowledge production.

Introduction

Much has been written and critiqued about the importance of generating sound knowledge management systems in order that countries develop effective and integrated economies in a global world (World Bank 1998; Clarke 2001). This has also been true for the education sector, particularly as education has been considered to lay the foundation for other fields (King 1991). Governments have been urged to develop better knowledge bases for determining educational policy and practice in an increasingly interconnected world. However, the rate, quality and success in knowledge creation and its application have been judged as being relatively low in the education sector compared with other sectors (Organisation for Economic Cooperation and Development [OECD] 2000).

In response to such calls, there has been a recognition within the educational community in the UK of the requirement to explore how to build effective research capacity and improve research quality in this sector. To this end, and with varying degrees of success, there has been an assortment of initiatives (National Education Research Forum [NERF] 1999–2006) that have attempted to map patterns of research activity and capacity across the UK in order to oversee the development of a coherent strategy for education research and its use. The most recent of these is the Strategic

Forum for Research in Education (SFRE), which will run over a three-year period and aims systematically to consider the ongoing challenges facing educational research capacity in the UK now and in the future. In attempting to build an overall strategy for UK educational research, what has been refreshing about SFRE is its recognition that it is essential to pay attention to the particularities, issues and challenges that arise in each of the four nations (England, Scotland, Wales and Northern Ireland) with regard to building research capacity.

Arguably, there is as much that separates as unites the four jurisdictions in the 'United' Kingdom in terms of research capacity building in education. While Crossley and Holmes (2001) assert that local issues cannot be understood without reference to the global context in educational research capacity building, it could equally be argued that national problems of capacity building cannot be realistically considered without an understanding of local differences, priorities, and agendas.

This paper aims to provide some understanding of the particularities of research capacity building in the Northern Ireland (NI) context by exploring its distinctive socio-historical context, and analysing the consequences of it being a small polity, with the intention that this argumentation may be transferred to other inter/national contexts. Unlike the remaining jurisdictions of the UK, there is at present little in the way of specific initiatives that directly or systematically aim to enhance research capacity in teacher education, outside particular institutional support. Thus, this discussion locates issues related to teacher education within more generic concerns for research capacity building in NI and seeks to problematise any notion of an easy transfer of strategies from elsewhere to the local context. Instead, a perspective is adopted that the NI education research and policy communities, while benefiting from these initiatives, should capitalise on emergent, collaborative relationships and build a fit-for-purpose strategy based on an analysis of NI's actual educational research priorities, as well as its deficits and strengths with respect to research capability. The paper concludes with a showcase of four areas of distinctive research capacity development in NI that could be harnessed to contribute to a more cohesive research strategy for education in a new socio-political and economic era.

Understanding research capacity building in the NI context

There is no agreed definition of what we mean by 'research capacity' never mind the best means by which to build this within the education sector. In technical terms, we refer most frequently to two main dimensions: (1) the numbers of active or potentially active researchers and (2) the range of the methodological skill-set available to engage in fit-for-purpose education research. Clearly these dimensions are important and need to be taken into consideration as indicated, on the one hand, by the demographic downturn in educational research (Lawn and Furlong 2007; Pollard 2008) – we are getting older, greyer and there are fewer of us – and, on the other, by the various critiques on quality – which have tended to focus on concerns of methodological robustness and the paucity of quantitative research in particular (Tooley and Darby 1998). Indeed, in NI, both these weaknesses in research capacity have been identified, characterised by the small numbers of educational researchers coming through and the restricted range of research skills available (Gardner and Gallagher 2007; Leitch 2008).

Notwithstanding this definition, Munn (2007, 2008) suggests that research capacity building is not simply about the supply side, it is also about the capacity of commissioners and users of research to understand and draw on existing research and in Schuller's (2007, 3) words 'to be able to formulate effective demands for further research'. Thus, we need to critique the notion of what we mean by 'educational capacity building' and widen it to include not simply the acquisition of methodological skills and capacities by educational researchers but also the understanding of the range and purposes of these by policy makers and other user/stakeholder groups, including the improvement of the public understanding of research and its applications.

While welcoming this expanded definition that should lead to increased sustainability, education researchers need to be watchful of unwittingly tying research capacity building too neatly into some form of instrumental accountability in the service of policy-making and public funding agendas (see Oancea [2005] on the 'new orthodoxy'). In a country the size of NI, with its history of political dysfunction and disconnection, developing links between research, policy and practice should undoubtedly be welcomed as a core priority in terms of research capacity building. This is perhaps especially so as NI emerges uneasily from its prolonged period of political conflict and, thus, building a collaborative community is one of the present and continuing aspirations for this region. Those involved in education in NI have arrived at a point of recognition that for educational research to flourish, we need to adopt an increased openness to collaboration and to developing intelligent research communities that strengthen policy-oriented research capacity and lead to more robust evidence bases for educational decision-making and action. However, as an emergent community, we will also need to ensure we keep thinking 'outside the box'. Our understanding of capacity building must also keep its sights upon the vital importance of valuing and supporting innovation, problem-definition, creativity and 'blue skies thinking' within research possibilities. In this new era for NI, if research is truly to transform education and, ultimately, be integral to the knowledge economy of the country then it is also vital to extend the boundaries of what are considered appropriate methodologies and dissemination for differing purposes and to differing ends (OECD 2004).

Research capacity in teacher education and the quantity versus quality debate

As traditional knowledge institutions, universities are considered central to increasingly knowledge-based societies (Etzkowitz et al. 2000). This positioning is not unproblematic, especially as it pertains to the education sector and the ways in which, for example, the mechanics of accountability may militate against how knowledge is generated, mediated, integrated and accrued.

NI is served by two universities, both of which supply teacher education and training through schools of education and both of which are research active. Additionally, there are two university colleges providing teacher education that also contribute to the educational research knowledge base. In the recent (2008) UK Research Assessment Exercise (RAE), three of the four higher education institutions (HEIs) were returned for assessment and, given their previous starting points, all three performed relatively successfully on grade average as an estimate of research quality (where 'grade average' is a measure of quantum of researchers submitted × rated quality of individual papers per unit of assessment), but with relatively small numbers of active researchers. In fact, the total number of returns in NI has not quite been sustained from the previous 2001 Exercise (*n*=39). Despite one university college submitting a return to the 2008 RAE, an addition to the 2001 Exercise, only 38 research-active staff were included from NI HEIs in the 2008 Education Unit of Assessment; one down on the 2001 entry. While this is comparable to Wales' 37 (77 in 2001) who have also slumped, it is underwhelming in contrast to the development in Scotland with 258 returned (compared with 162 in the 2001 round).

In terms of research capacity, this is a somewhat unsatisfactory profile, given the actual numbers of academics involved in teacher education and the commitment in this context to ensure education is a research-informed profession. Despite sustained attempts and financial investment by the two universities to increase the quantum of research active staff in education in the seven years between the two research assessment exercises, this evident lack of improvement suggests something of a systemic problem. Clearly, the particular challenge of attracting and retaining high quality, national and international researchers in a small country emerging from civil strife is one important dimension of this concern. However, wider issues need also to be considered; some of which may have connection with and relevance to, other small nations.

Reflection on how to build and sustain capacity in NI also raises the predicament about the complex and potentially inverse relationship between the drive for increased capacity, on the one hand, and, on the other, the drive for high quality, as currently defined within the high-stakes, UK RAE, and where the outcome is directly linked to core research funding for HEIs. This drive towards achieving a high quality rating often involves universities taking a calculated decision to return a highly selective and small number of research-active, high-quality, staff as safe bets, in order to be assured of success in the final educational research league tables. The tragedy of this tactic, for tactics are surely the name of the research assessment game, is that the remainder of colleagues subsequently become labelled 'not-research active'. Such a label becomes an identity straitjacket from which it is increasingly difficult to escape, given that the consequences of not being 'RAE returned' commonly means less access to significant levels of university support for researcher development and professional renewal. Whilst not a generality, the evidence is there that many HEIs have elected for this calculation in the recent UK RAE, and the case for NI is little different. Seventy percent of the total university returns to the RAE for education had fewer than 20 staff and there was a decrease of 18% in total volume across the UK from the 2001 to the 2008 RAE. Arguably, however, the consequences for a small country's knowledge economy and capacity building are significantly augmented.

Thus, while Schuller (2007) argues that to some extent, the two dimensions – quality and quantity – in educational research are independent of one another and that it is possible for a country to score highly on one but not the other, the penalties for not attending to and strengthening research capacity that has impact within that country's educational system nevertheless seem obvious. For now, it is crucially important for NI to raise its standards and capacity for high-quality educational research however complex the task, particularly if educational researchers wish to play an influential role in improving the knowledge base for the education system in this new era.

Additionally, in a relatively delimited socio-economic and geographic context sustaining two universities, it is difficult to get away from the harsh realities of a competitive market mentality. While Peters (2003, 373) posits that competition is necessary for a successful knowledge economy, such a statement flies in the face of collaboration being central to the acquisition of social capital, as reflected in many of the recent attempts to conceptualise research capacity building (Fowler and Procter 2009).

This contradiction may be particularly problematic in a small polity, such as NI. The high stakes of the RAE, the importance of prestige and esteem indicators and, where core funding follows achievement, the drive to compete and win publicly-funded research contracts can significantly outweigh academics' willingness to co-operate, even when joint research ventures might significantly improve research quality. While some good examples of collaborative practice between educational researchers in the two universities can be celebrated in NI, such as Gallagher and Smith's work (2000a, 2000b, 2000c) on the effects of the selective system of secondary education in NI, nevertheless the fundamental tension between rivalry and partnership generally undermines a genuine and fuller commitment to sustained collaborative research activity. This issue of competition may well exist elsewhere in the UK (and indeed, on occasion, between the four nations) in relation to imperatives over economic advantage, league tables and winning successful funding – factors that rupture collaboration and seriously need to be taken into consideration in any deliberations towards a national strategy for research capacity building.

Socio-historical context: size matters

NI is distinctive from the other three jurisdictions (England, Scotland and Wales) by virtue of it having a very small population of approximately 1.7 million. Although focusing largely on the international development of research capacity and quality in small countries, Crossley and Holmes (2001) define a 'small state' as one not dissimilar in size to that of NI, with populations *c.* 1.5 million. They argue that smallness of size has major implications for capacity building and that care should be taken by small states not to import or imitate uncritically models of educational research capacity building that are shown to be successful elsewhere. Rather, efforts to strengthen research capacity 'must give attention to the distinctive "social ecology" of small states' (Crossley and Holmes 2001, 403) and innovations need to be well-attuned to the needs, values and cultures of the local context.

While the development context that Crossley and Holmes (2001) refer to may differ, the principles in relation to NI would seem to have significant application. Gardner and Gallagher (2007) described the approach to educational research in NI as 'ad hoc' and fragmented, with no discernible and co-ordinated strategy. On the face of it, given its size (geographic and demographic), this observation, although accurate, seems absurd; however, given its educational complexity and the internal political tensions that have persisted, this is perhaps not so inexplicable. The social ecology of this small country has been severely affected by 40 years of political strife and divisiveness, a situation that has led to the relationship between key stakeholder groups in education, particularly the policy-makers and educational researchers, suffering from what might be described as an insidious form of estrangement. Given its intimate size, most educationists in NI (policy-makers, inspectorate, teachers, advisers, teacher educators and researchers) are well known to each other and have often enjoyed a high degree of social ease and rapport over the years. Until fairly recently, this was often in sharp contrast to the apparently intractable and convoluted nature of formal discussions and dialogue about the possibilities for improving and investing in the relationship between policy, research and practice, which mostly ended in deadlock.

During periods of direct rule by the UK government in the 1980s and 1990s, dilemmas arose due to various, local responses to direct policy transfer of education policy from the UK to NI. Specifically, attempts by local politicians to ameliorate, by means of 'policy slippage' and/or 'policy discretion' the worst excesses of direct rule meant that it was often difficult to retain a close or transparent relationship between the educational research and policy communities.

Indeed, given the political complexity and sensitivities of these times, the notion of an accumulating or shared corpus of research-based knowledge to inform educational decision-making and practice development in NI was an unlikely aspiration. Local politicians and policy-makers were highly sensitive to the perennial problems associated with religious and identity affiliations, the lack of political consensus, perceived differences in educational priorities and thus the potential political repercussions of adopting recommendations based on research evidence. Appeasing traditionally powerful vested interests in this context often meant that rational educational decision-making based on knowledge had to give way to political expediency (see McMinn and Phoenix [2005] for a fuller discussion). Moreover, in some instances, empirical knowledge could not easily be brought to bear on policy developments. Thus ideological appeasement rather than veracity of evidence frequently tipped the balance when it came to the thorny issues of policy and practice. A *cause célèbre* is *Chocolate cream soldiers*, an ethnographic evaluation of a cultural studies project undertaken in NI schools, during the 1970s (O'Connor 1980). Due to the sponsors feeling undermined by some of the critical, political insinuations reflected in the final report, the evaluation team was purportedly 'all-but-instructed not to present its data' (Jenkins 1984, 241). However, academic publication of a paper based on the data could not ultimately be suppressed.

Another more recent example is typified by Gardner and Cowan's (2000, 2005) studies on the validity and reliability of the Transfer Procedure Test in NI. The Transfer Test is a high-stakes test taken by children of around 11 years of age who wish to attend grammar schools in NI. This was the largest independent and technical study of the Test ever conducted. The researchers found that the Transfer Test did not meet the requirements of the international standards on educational testing (American Educational Research Association, American Psychological Association and National Council on Measurement 1999), and had significant flaws in relation to its predictive power and its potential for significant grade misclassification of children, with detrimental consequences for children in the middle–lower-band grades who were likely to miss out on grammar school selection. After an initial denial, the Department of Education and Curriculum Council for Examinations and Assessment accepted that the Test was 'fundamentally flawed', yet, it is only in the most recent and still vituperative public debate on abolition of selection at 11 that this test has finally been abolished, almost nine years after the research evidence was presented.

Until recently, these unwarranted tensions and contentions affected the relationships that could legitimately be developed between research partners in the educational endeavour, in this relatively small local context. However, with the advent of a peace agreement two important changes are worth noting. First, a slowly evolving political devolution was reintroduced in May 2007 and this has resulted in significant differences in the political and legal landscape from the rest of the UK, notably regarding education. Second, a recent review of public administration has provided an opportunity to prune and revitalise public services in NI, making a public sector that is more accountable and encouraging of working together with a common purpose (Goldblatt McGuigan 2006). Together these initiatives have paved a way for a renewed set of researcher–policy-maker relations that could herald a fresh epoch of dialogue about the potentially positive relationship between educational research and policy development in producing, sharing mediating and using knowledge and the vital role of research capacity building in achieving this.

Despite the very particular political undertones that suffuse education discourse in NI, other small polities give witness to similar tensions and solutions and, it could be argued that a necessary but not unique function of small states is that they must stabilise working relationships in order to find a way to accommodate evidence without wreaking systemic disturbances. A relevant comparison arises in Scotland, where periodically the issue of continuing interference of the Catholic Church surfaces as a source of tension between Left and Right and between various kinds of extremists (Conroy 2008). Evidence is adduced for both perspectives and put in the public domain but studiously ignored because the political sensitivities are too great and the potential consequences too significant.

Capacity initiatives: learning from the field

Thus far, in NI, we have not had an equivalent financial investment in the development of research capacity building for teacher education equivalent to what exists in the other parts of the UK. Thus, in Scotland the Applied Educational Research Scheme (AERS) supports a national approach to research capacity building which involved an investment of £2 million over a five-year programme funded by the Scottish Funding Council and the Scottish Executive Education Department (Baird and Baron 2009). Wales has the benefit of the Welsh Educational Research Network (WERN), funded to provide a pilot capacity building network from October 2007–June 2008, and all 10 Welsh HEIs with education or related departments are committed to building collaboration by participating in the scheme (Davies and Salisbury 2009). In England the Teacher Education Research Network (TERN) aims to establish a regional network for education research capacity building in the north-west of England to kick start or augment the local developing educational research capacity.

From the NI standpoint, the educational research community here tends to look 'in on' or 'across the water' at these initiatives with various degrees of envy, delight and scepticism. These initiatives have been based loosely on concepts arising from social capital theory (Putnam 1995; Nahapiet and Ghoshal 1998) which emphasise the added value of interpersonal relationships and networking and, according to Fowler and Procter (2009), provide a means of taking account of the interlinked notions of building the research capacity of the individual researcher and building the research capacity of the wider research community. Thus, investment in these initiatives has been focused on the generation of increased collaboration, developing networks and the engagement of those participating in the 'working and/or social practices' of research-in-action. In turn, this process is argued to foster increased skill, improved research outputs and, ultimately, increased numbers of quality researchers.

While it remains early days to judge the long-term impact of each of these investments for local research capacity building, early evaluations of AERS and

WERN (TERN has only been initiated since November 2008 and, thus, has not yet undergone an evaluation) have tended to be largely inwardly focused, self-referential evaluations (Gardner 2008 on WERN; Rees et al. 2007; Baird and Baron 2009 on AERS), where, in the final analysis, those participating deem themselves to have benefited from engaging in these research capacity building initiatives. Specifically, it is argued that the benefits have been much wider than simply the professional skills enhancement of individual teacher educators (although this has been overwhelmingly identified by participants surveyed in both the case of AERS and WERN as being of immense importance), extending to claims of increased inter-institutional collaboration in the case of WERN (Davies and Salisbury 2009) and the co-production of knowledge between academics and other stakeholders in education for AERS (Munn and Baron 2008; Baird and Baron 2009).

The real test in the longer term, however, for the effectiveness of such initiatives in building local capacity needs to take account of tangible and sustained outcomes as well as relationship building and process-oriented cultures of participation. For instance, in Scotland, it remains an open question as to whether the £2 million of investment in pursuit of capacity building networks through AERS is deemed value for money, particularly when institutions outside the lead institutions appear to have built capacity, and indeed capacity and quality as evidenced by the recent (2008) RAE, without such financial investment.

Moreover, in evaluating overall impact, account must be taken of how such collective enterprises can unwittingly create potential 'outgroups'. Despite the capability of initiatives such as AERS, WERN, TERN and the Teaching and Learning Research Programme (TLRP – a major UK research capacity building initiative funded by the Economic and Social Research Council, the Higher Education Funding Council for England, the Department for Education and Science, the Scottish Executive, the National Assembly for Wales and the NI Executive to enhance research-based practice in teaching and learning that ran from 2001 to 2009) to 'bond' social capital (after Putnam 1995) and, indeed, in many instances, to 'bridge' social capital between researchers and organisations, the 'shadow' side of such collectives is that they can inadvertently inhibit capacity-growth by alienating those teacher educators/researchers outside the boundaries of the initiative, who have not directly benefited from the investment. Those alienated, through not being part of the 'club', can consciously or unconsciously undermine development through disinterest and cynical disengagement from dissemination events intended as opportunities for knowledge transfer and capacity building.

Thus, the NI educational research community has a lot to be cautious of as well as inspired by through the initiatives achieved elsewhere in the UK (via WERN, AERS, TERN and, even TLRP). Given NI's particular ecology, its location and scale, it is unlikely that any model derived elsewhere, successful by whatever standards, can readily be transferred wholesale to this context.

Developing capacity: new beginnings and the limits of 'social contract'

In the past year, the NI Education Research Forum (NIERF) has been inaugurated, stimulated, in this instance perhaps, atypically by one of the two government departments concerned with education in NI (the Department of Education [DE], responsible for schools, and the Department for Employment and Learning [DEL], responsible for third-level education, training and a range of employment-related matters). Due to a shift in government planning, and the demands for evidence-based policy-making, the DE recognised its own need for a more co-ordinated approach to educational research. It responded by initiating the Forum, gathering together various stakeholders, including the HEIs, with the goal of exploring the potential for knowledge-sharing as a first step towards better strategic development for knowledge-generation. The objectives of NIERF are to provide opportunities to develop a discourse on educational research that has been hitherto missing or ruptured and, in so doing, to explore the potential for developing an agreed, coherent strategy for educational research and the infrastructure and capacity that would be needed to support this for the coming period. At this juncture, although set to expand, NIERF comprises member representatives from each of the HEIs, the Education and Training Inspectorate (ETI), and the two departments with responsibility for education (DE and DEL).

It is early days yet to assess whether or not this new forum, initiated top-down, with as yet no financial investment, but palpable good will, can agree on and deliver a cohesive strategy, which will lead to significant change in the face of the educational issues confronting NI in the next period. First steps have included a mapping exercise to tie in with the UK SFRE agenda and a planned series of local symposia hosted with key stakeholder groups, including policy-makers and practitioners, to establish an understanding of the various perspectives on purposes, methodologies, needs and priorities for educational research in this locale. By comparison to each of the initiatives in Scotland, Wales and England, this is on a significantly different scale of investment, financial or otherwise. Nevertheless, this development, like the others, is underpinned by the implicit belief in the value of dialogue and processes that build and/or bridge social capital in order to deliver educational outcomes. Within the current political climate and, after four decades of 'turmoil and fragmentation' (Haire 2009), there is an appetite by many in the education profession for more open, transparent relationships. Presently, this development is being welcomed widely as a 'new beginning' with definite opportunities for research capacity building as central to the agenda.

Furlong and Oancea (2005) argue for a new 'social contract' between educational researchers, funders and non-academic users of research, bringing them into closer contact, and with the need for research to be more closely allied to educational policy problem-solving. Certainly on the face of it, this seems a reasonable and mutually beneficial aspiration within NI, but the extent to which improved partnerships are possible, as stimulated by NIERF, will depend on political (in every sense) will, an openness in dialogue, flexibility and an increased understanding of the issues and complexities involved for all parties. There is certainly plenty to focus on in terms of negotiating a shared agenda from the list of priorities facing education in this location and listed within the Minister of Education's strategy and the DEL strategic plan (2006–2009). Specific challenges to be addressed include pressures for rationalisation of school provision, reducing the achievement gap, broader entitlement, improved access to high-quality education, effective school leadership, economic contribution of further education, priority skills areas, inclusion and ways of achieving greater social equality. In order satisfactorily to meet these expectations, there is a need to increase or amass the evidence base on many aspects of education around strategic priorities and, to achieve this, a strong, vibrant research community is necessary.

It is important to recognise that this Forum aims to create and operationalise a renewed form of 'social contract' for research in NI, based on networking, dialogue and decision-making. In this sense alone, it is characteristically rather different from the other three countries' initiatives on research capacity, which were stimulated more directly from concerns by academics and researchers themselves. Primarily, NIERF is derived as a result of a proactive move by a government department and as such could be viewed cynically as instrumental, driven strictly by its own strategic interests, something all partners involved may need to be vigilant of. In response to Furlong and Oancea (2005), Hammersley (2008) challenges the desirability of a closer relationship between research and policy-making processes, cautioning that pressures for a new social contract can too easily displace academic research, making it subordinate to policy-making and thereby undermining the professionalism of educational researchers. Thus, observing NIERF as it develops, we must be cautious in NI, not to become so locked into national policy constructions and their ideological narratives to such a degree that we become 'servants of the state… and have no time for informed critique or of perceiving the social consequences of the policy' Peters (2001, 12).

Nonetheless, despite these cautionary tales, it behoves all parties involved at this juncture in NI to take the risk of authentic yet watchful engagement and view the advent of NIERF as a timely opportunity for building research capacity at a systemic level. This may yet promote new forms of collaboration, improved infrastructure, increased research investment and thus enhanced research capacity in its wider conceptualisation. Clearly, it is early days yet to assess whether or not the recently instituted forum, NIERF, will adequately meet its aspirations to create a sound knowledge base, sustained in large measure by 'home grown' research for the education system in NI. Feedback from ongoing multi-level evaluation should however tell the tale for the future.

Learning from within: harnessing assets and potentialities

It would be remiss to suggest somehow that this government-led initiative, NIERF, represents the singular most important feature in NI's landscape of educational research capacity building. Undoubtedly, it is seen as importantly positioned and with opportunities for two-way learning from its strategic relationship with SFRE. Nevertheless, during the recent timeframe, there have been a number of positive sites of organic development within NI that are also worthy of highlighting and that form part of the overall geography of educational research. A number of these has been pioneered through academic initiative and enterprise, while others are more directly the result of ideological commitment and, still others, the consequence of the particular historical and geo-political positioning of NI. Four main areas of research capacity development will be synopsised, with each one having something to say about the strengths and potentialities that are being consolidated in this locale, while simultaneously echoing various issues and challenges of broader significance on the theme of research capacity building.

Celebrating research distinctiveness: education and conflict

There is substantial potential to capitalise upon the distinctiveness of NI, turning the negatives of recent times to our own and others' benefit and advantage, in terms of developing research of international significance that arises from particular local concerns. By dint of its history and the sustained civil and political conflict, NI has developed as a site of international expertise in understanding education and conflict and peace education, and reconciliation and human rights in post-conflict societies, all of which amounts to an 'emerging field' of interest (UNICEF 2006). Both universities have centres of research excellence, which have built strong international collaboration on the basis of research knowledge accumulated on these internationally critical issues. For instance, the UNESCO centre based at the University of Ulster was established in 2001 and has been recognised for its contributions to research on development education, pluralism, human rights and democracy. Additionally, the Joint Learning Initiative on Children and Ethnic Diversity (JLICED) based at Queen's University represents a global initiative bringing together over 60 leading researchers, policy-makers and practitioners worldwide. It works in partnership with local organisations in regions characterised by ethnic divisions and conflict to help develop innovative and effective early childhood programmes aimed at building more inclusive communities.

Although the total scale of NI scholars contributing to this area of research worldwide might be considered slight, the methodological expertise accrued, the analytical tools developed and the impact of published outcomes internationally should not be underestimated. In this way, research capacity building, whilst vital for local knowledge economies must also be viewed as transcending local boundaries with contributions that strengthen global research capacity and knowledge accumulation.

Capitalising on methodological expertise: baseline evaluation and randomised control trials (RCTs)

The NFER@ Queen's (National Foundation for Educational Research at Queen's University Belfast Centre for Educational Research) was an innovative partnership, established in 2001, between a university school of education and a major national research body. Its goal and specialism resided in various forms of applied research to meet the evidence needs of policy-makers in NI. Building on its initial success with over £6 million accrued in research income, including major support from the Atlantic Philanthropies Foundation, this became an independent, multidisciplinary Centre for Effective Education (CEE) in 2008. Its forte now lies in evaluating the effectiveness of educational programmes and interventions and, in particular, the Centre has gained considerable expertise over the past few years in designing and running RCTs and quasi-experimental evaluations. CEE's research staff is set to increase to 18 full-time researchers and it is currently running over 15 major studies, of which nine are RCTs, still considered by many to be the 'gold standard' of robustness for educational researchers. The Centre considers itself to be running more RCTs in education than any other educational research centre in Ireland and indeed in the UK. Nurturing such methodological and statistical expertise has undoubtedly addressed some prior local, and indeed inter/national capacity concerns (OECD 2003), in terms of quantitative skills sets available. In the discourse of the knowledge economy, this accruing methodological resource is an example that may also be exportable to researchers elsewhere in the UK and beyond.

Integrating and supporting practitioner research

As Richardson (1994, 5) indicated some time ago, in the North American context: 'In a widespread shift, the conception of teachers as merely consumers of educational research is changing to one of teachers as producers and mediators of educational knowledge'. In order to build the fullest most inclusive working model of educational research capacity in NI, practitioner research needs to contribute visibly to the overall quantum and quality of research output. Practitioner research in NI has been significantly underdeveloped, under-recognised and, until recently, uncoordinated in terms of its contribution to knowledge production, teacher development and school improvement (Leitch 2008). Teacher research in NI is promoted in a number of ways and by a variety of stakeholders (e.g., through university teacher education programmes; curriculum advisory and support services, teacher development initiatives, bursaries and so on). Nevertheless, teacher research has never enjoyed the support and infrastructure that has been available and continues to be evident in other parts of the UK (e.g. National Teacher Research Panel [England]; Best Practice Research Awards [DfES]; Networked Learning Communities [National College of School Leadership]; Chartered Teacher Programme [Scotland]).

Sensitive to this deficit, the General Teaching Council for Northern Ireland (GTCNI), established as recently as 2000, strongly promotes a policy of teaching as a 'research-driven', and 'research-informed' profession. Viewing practitioner research as central, GTCNI has, in addition to many other initiatives, supported the development of a digital repository (Access to Research Resources for Teachers Space (ARRTS)) to ensure access and dissemination of local practitioner research, including teacher action research and high standard master's and doctoral thesis research. Part of the vision is that the database will contribute to evidence-informed practice and policy-making in education and encourage a partnership between the local educational research community and practicing teachers. While still largely aspirational, this move undoubtedly advocates and values practitioner research in a way that has not previously been evident. In truth, however, much wider support is needed for legitimising the knowledge-generating potential of the range of teacher research and developing a workable means for supporting and integrating systematically the processes and outcomes into the profession's evidence pool, if it is not to remain an 'unworked mine' (Dewey 1929) of local educational intelligence.

Looking to the future, a significant element of any comprehensive strategy for building educational research capacity in NI should take advantage of the global shift that is occurring in relation to practitioner research and, in so doing, galvanise and capitalise on this undervalued resource within the field.

Looking South to build capacity

Finally, any attempt to situate NI educational research capacity building without taking account of its relationship with the South, the Republic of Ireland (RoI), itself the western fringe of the European Union (EU), would be seriously remiss. NI has not simply focused its gaze on research initiatives and directions arising in the other three jurisdictions of the UK, but has paid attention to the bigger international picture through capitalising on its relationship and links with its adjoining EU neighbour.

There are seven universities in the South of Ireland and a range of colleges of education engaged in basic and applied research, which are overseen by the Higher

Education Authority (HEA – the statutory planning and development body for higher education and research in Ireland). Despite the speed and depth of the current financial crisis worldwide, nowhere felt more sharply than in the RoI, where it has been described as a 'Titanic-like shipwreck' (*Irish Times* 2009), a sum of nearly £2 billion has been allocated for research, technological development and innovation, and of this amount, £550 million was allocated to strengthen the breadth and quality of research capacity in higher education (National Development Plan 2000–2006). Whilst it is difficult to anticipate the full repercussions of the financial downturn on universities in the RoI, and the impact specifically of investment in educational research, nevertheless, it is clear that boosting academic research has been viewed as a high priority in upholding Ireland's knowledge economy and education specifically.

Along with strategic objectives surrounding improved cross-border relationships in building a peaceful future, research investment is reflected directly in a number of additional ventures that explicitly promote the value of a coordinated approach to building research capacity North and South. Irish President, Mary McAleese has launched a development education initiative that brings together all nine universities in the Republic and NI with universities in four countries in sub-Saharan Africa to make an effective contribution to poverty reduction, and research in education is a central concern to the international venture (Walshe 2009).

More specifically, the Standing Conference for Teacher Education North and South (SCoTENS), set up in 2003, directly builds cross-border research capacity in teacher education by awarding small annual 'seed funding' for research and conference projects from colleges of education and HEI education departments on the 'island of Ireland' and which are generated by a North–South partnership. Additionally a number of specific SCoTENS-supported research capacity initiatives have provided added value, such as a joint venture convened by the Educational Studies Association for Ireland (ESAI) and the British Educational Research Association (BERA); more recently, an all-Ireland capacity building project to support and develop arts-based educational research (ABER) has been inaugurated. Although the long-term sustainability of many of these projects is questionable, and few have led on to major research grant applications by teacher educators, nevertheless SCoTENS has supported a broad range of significant collaborative projects in such areas as digital recording and information and communication technology, autism, citizenship education, science education, social justice and teacher development. All of these directly and/or indirectly have added to the quantum of knowledge, led to increased capacity building and opened up lines of communication and professional development within teacher education both sides of the 'border' that otherwise would not have happened. In the longer term, in order to extend research capacity in teacher education, what is required is something more deliberate and sustained in NI that extends beyond and incorporates some of the successes achieved through SCoTENS.

Joining up the dots and harnessing the slipstream

Despite what might be interpreted as a generally gloomy view within the early sections of this paper, these four areas of ongoing research development act as counterpoint, highlighting NI's initiative, strengths and possibilities in educational research. The evidence base in NI has undeniably benefited from a number of disparate streams of input and investment and educational researchers, including those in teacher education, have been inspired to respond creatively and, consequently, are contributing to producing new knowledge that is being recognised locally, nationally and internationally. Hand in hand with this goes a range of ESRC/TLRP-funded projects, an ESRC Regional Training Centre (2006–2008) and ESRC Placement Fellowship Scheme, all of which add to a rich tapestry of research activity, networks and collaboration that are surely building research capacity through accumulating social and knowledge capital here.

So, if there's a problem, what is it, one might ask. Despite all this endeavour, how can it be that many of the indicators for burgeoning research capacity are not obviously being significantly advanced in NI? Analysis of the problem is complex, as indicated from earlier discussion, but, at least in significant measure, is inherent in the fragmentation and balkanisation that characterises much educational research activity here. Rich pockets of research activity and expertise exist within the education system but little of this is 'joined up', and with no single body or 'evidence centre' holding an awareness or record of the overall contribution to knowledge and how accumulated wisdom might be used to best effect.

By any calculation, NI is a small state and with this comes various systemic strengths and challenges that must be understood and faced locally rather than looking to emulate what has been adduced as successful elsewhere in the UK. While we have much to learn and tap into from the slipstream of initiatives and external expertise that has been created by such research capacity building catalysts as AERS, WERN and TERN etc, NI's educational research and policy communities presently need to address the issue of co-ordination. Without some overarching means to channel and join up the plethora of contributions to evidence and research activity and some significant investment in this co-ordination, much of the cumulative impact of knowledge generated will continue to be lost to the system, few economies of scale can be made, and opportunities for consolidation of local expertise will dissipate. Given the urgency of some of the educational priorities facing NI, not to develop such coordination would represent a significant and missed opportunity.

Conclusion: towards a future for research capacity in NI

Significantly, NI is a society in transition, emerging from a prolonged period of conflict and political volatility but with ongoing concerns for the stability and longevity of the hard-won peace. Given the current patterns and infrastructure, there is an imperative to invest in building and extending research capacity, and this will mean increasing numbers of methodologically sound and versatile researchers while simultaneously committing to an expanded version and understanding of research capacity building based on a dialogue between the government, the researcher community, practitioners and the public. The recently established Forum (NIERF), drawing on the groundwork of the SFRE, is set to have a significant role to play in this process.

In recognition of the spirit of a new political era in NI (NI/UK Government 2005, section 2.4), a collaborative coalition that involves teachers and teacher educators with other stakeholders in forms of democratic participation and control, in defining educational problems to be studied, setting research priorities, and in determining how the results are to be used and disseminated, would be a far-sighted, if challenging, development but one worthy of investment, if we are to take charge of our own education destiny.

References

American Educational Research Association, American Psychological Association and National Council on Measurement. 1999. *Education standards for educational and psychological testing.* Washington, DC: APA.

Baird, A., and S. Baron. 2009. Research capacity building: A Scottish model. Paper presented to the American Educational Research Association, San Diego Keynote Symposium: 'Capacity building evaluations, initiatives and obstacles across the UK: Reflections from England, Scotland, Wales and Northern Ireland', April 17, San Diego, USA.

Clarke, T. 2001. The knowledge economy. *Journal of Education and Training* 43, nos. 4–5: 189–96.

Conroy, J. 2008. Sectarianism and Scottish education. In *Scottish education.* 3rd ed., ed. T. Bryce and W. Hulmes, 793–803. Edinburgh, UK: Edinburgh University Press.

Crossley, M., and K. Holmes. 2001. Challenges for educational research: International development, partnerships and capacity building in small states. *Oxford Review of Education* 27, no. 3: 395–409.

Davies, S., and J. Salisbury. 2009. Reflections based on the evaluations of the Welsh Education Research Network. Paper presented to American Educational Research Association, San Diego Keynote Symposium: 'Capacity building evaluations, initiatives and obstacles across the UK: Reflections from England, Scotland, Wales and Northern Ireland', April 17.

Dewey, J. 1929. *The sources of a science of education.* New York: Liverright.

Etzkowitz, H., A. Webster, C. Geghardt, B. Regina, and C. Terra. 2000. The future of university and the university of the future: Evolution of ivory tower to entrepreneurial paradigm. *Research Policy* 29, no. 2: 313–30.

Fowler, Z., and R. Procter. 2009. Personalising capacity: How might we strategise for the capacity building of individuals? Reflections from an evaluation of TLRP research projects. Paper presented to American Educational Research Association, San Diego Keynote Symposium: 'Capacity building evaluations, initiatives and obstacles across the UK: Reflections from England, Scotland, Wales and Northern Ireland', April 17.

Furlong, J., and A. Oancea. 2005. *Assessing quality in applied and practice-based educational research: A framework for discussion.* Oxford, UK: Oxford Department of Educational Studies. http://www.esrcsocietytoday.ac.uk/ESRCInfoCentre/Images/assessing_quality_shortreport_tcm6-8232.pdf

Gallagher, A., and A. Smith. 2000a. SEL1.1: Overview paper. In *The effects of the selective system of secondary education in Northern Ireland.* Vol. 1, ed. A. Gallagher and A. Smith, 11. Bangor, UK: Department of Education.

Gallagher, A., and A. Smith. 2000b. *The effects of the selective system of secondary education in Northern Ireland: Main report.* Bangor, UK: Department of Education.

Gallagher, A., and A. Smith. 2000c. *The effects of the selective system of secondary education in Northern Ireland: Briefing paper.* Bangor, UK: Department of Education.

Gardner, J. 2008. *Welsh education research network: An evaluation.* Belfast, NI: Queens University.

Gardner, J., and P. Cowan. 2000. Testing the test: A study of the reliability and validity of the Northern Ireland transfer procedure test in enabling the selection of pupils for grammar school places. http://arrts.gtcni.org.uk/gtcni/bitstream/2428/6312/1/Testing%20the%20Test.pdf (accessed April 29, 2009).

Gardner, J., and P. Cowan. 2005. The fallibility of high stakes '11+' testing in Northern Ireland. *Assessment in Education* 12, no 2: 145–65.

Gardner, J., and T. Gallagher. 2007. Gauging the deliverable? Educational research in Northern Ireland. *European Educational Research Journal* 6, no. 1: 101–14.

Goldblatt McGuigan. 2006. *Office of the First Minister and Deputy First Minister: International research project – 'Moving to common boundaries'*. Belfast, NI: Goldblatt McGuigan (in partnership with Social Research Centre, IRS and Mouchel Parkman). http://www.rpani.gov.uk/common_boundaries_final_report_goldblatt.pdf

Haire, W. 2009. Permanent Secretary for Education address to first symposium event for the Northern Ireland Education Research Forum, April 30, at Stranmillis University College, Belfast.

Hammersley, M. 2008. Troubling criteria: A critical commentary on Furlong and Oancea's framework for assessing educational research. *British Journal of Educational Research* 34no. 6: 747–62.

Irish Times. 2009. No time for whingers, January 3. http://www.irishtimes.com/newspaper/opinion/2009/0103/1230842387565.html

Jenkins, D. 1984. Chocolate cream soldiers: Sponsorship, ethnography and sectarianism. In *The research process in educational settings: Ten case studies,* ed. R. Burgess, 211–35. London: Falmer Press.

King, K. 1991. *Capacity building for educational research, planning and analysis: Summary implications for donors of a new aid strategy.* Edinburgh: University of Edinburgh.

Lawn, M., and J. Furlong, J. 2007. The social organisation of educational research in England. *European Education Research Journal* 6, no. 1: 55–70.

Leitch, R. 2008. Capacity and quality in education research in Northern Ireland: A stimulus report for the Strategic Forum for Research in Education. http://www.sfre.ac.uk/wp-content/uploads/2008/10/sfre-forum-1-reports-web.pdf pp73-123 (accessed April 12, 2009).

McMinn, R., and E. Phoenix. 2005. The Chilver report: Unity and diversity. *Irish Educational Studies* 14, no 1: 5–19.

Munn, P. 2007. Building research capacity collaboratively: Can we take ownership of our future? Presidential address at the British Educational Research Association Conference, 5–11 September, in London, UK.

Munn, P. 2008. Building research capacity collaboratively: Can we take ownership of our future? *British Educational Research Journal* 34, no. 4: 413–30.

Munn, P., and S. Baron. 2008. Research and practice. In *Scottish Education.* 3rd ed., ed. T. Bryce and W. Hulmes, 864–972. Edinburgh, UK: Edinburgh University Press.

Nahapiet, J., and S. Ghoshal. 1998. Social capital, intellectual capital, and the organisational advantage. *Academy of Management Review* 23, no. 2: 242–66.

NI/UK Government. 2005. A shared future: Policy and strategic framework for good relations in Northern Ireland. http://www.asharedfutureni.gov.uk/policy-strategic.pdf

O'Connor, S. 1980. Reports – 'Chocolate cream soldiers': Evaluating an experiment in non-sectarian education in Northern Ireland. *Curriculum Studies* 12, no. 3: 263–70.

Oancea, A. 2005. Criticisms of educational research: Key topics and levels of analysis. *British Educational Research Journal* 31, no. 2: 157–83.

Organisation for Economic Cooperation and Development. 2000. *A new economy?: The changing role of innovation and information technology in growth.* Paris: OECD Publishing.

Organisation for Economic Cooperation and Development. 2003. *New challenges for educational research.* Paris: OECD.

Organisation for Economic Cooperation and Development. 2004. *Knowledge management: Innovation in the knowledge economy implications for education and learning.* Paris: OECD Publishing.

Peters, M. 2001. National policy constructions of the knowledge economy: Towards a critique. *Journal of Educational Enquiry* 2, no. 1: 1–22.

Peters, M. 2003. Education policy in the age of knowledge capitalism. *Policy Futures in Education* 1, no. 3: 364–80.

Pollard, A. 2008. Towards new strategic initiatives for research capacity in education: A Discussion paper. *Building Research Capacity* 13: 1–6.

Putnam, R.D. 1995. Bowling alone: America's declining social capital. *Journal of Democracy* 6, no. 1: 64–78.

Rees, G., S. Baron, R. Boyask, and C. Taylor. 2007. Research-capacity building, professional learning and the social practices of research. *British Educational Research Journal* 33, no. 5: 761–79.

Richardson, V. 1994. Conducting research on practice. *Educational Researcher* 23, no. 5: 5–10.

Schuller, T. 2007. Capacity building in educational research: Sketching an international picture. http://74.125.77.132/search?q=cache:YVnTLAAIe_EJ:www.instytut.info/IIIkonf/referaty/3b/Schuller.pdf+Schuller+2007+research+capacityandcd=1andhl=enandct=clnkandgl=uk (accessed April 10, 2009).

Tooley, J., and D. Darby. 1998. *Educational research: A critique. A survey of published educational research.* London: Office for Standards in Education.

UNICEF. 2006. Basic education and gender equality. UNICEF at Oxford: Education experts confer on reaching children in conflicts. http://www.unicef.org/girlseducation/index_33249.html (accessed April 30, 2009).

Walshe, J. 2009. Africa–Ireland first five-nation project boosts research. *University World News,* April 27, Africa edition, Issue 0003.

World Bank. 1998. *World development report: 1998/9: Knowledge for development.* Washington DC: World Bank.

How engagement with research changes the professional practice of teacher-educators: a case study from the Welsh Education Research Network

Howard Tanner[a] and Susan M.B. Davies[b]

[a]*Centre for Research in Education, Swansea Metropolitan University, Swansea, UK;*
[b]*School of Education Studies and Social Inclusion, Trinity University College, University of Wales, Carmarthen, UK*

Learning to teach well is a complex task. Teacher-educators have a significant role to play in enabling students to reflect critically and analyse their own practice. However, there is a danger, as a result of funding pressures and other contrary factors, that many institutions that provide teacher education will become separated from their research base. The Welsh Education Research Network (WERN) is a pilot project funded by the Higher Education Funding Council in Wales and the Economic and Social Research Council with the aim of developing educational research capacity in Wales. This paper provides an analytical account of one research group of teacher-educators funded by WERN. The case study describes the research activity of the group and the views of its members on its impact for their professional practice. Finally an analysis of the findings concludes that engagement with research has resulted in positive changes to the knowledge, skills and critical awareness of the teacher-educators which has in turn brought benefits to the learning of their students.

Introduction

Learning to teach well is a complex task. Expert teaching performance depends on judgements made in the moment within a situation rather than the application of rules. Such judgements are difficult to observe and analyse and in consequence descriptions of expert teaching often over-emphasise more superficial features such as detailed lesson plans and clear objectives (Ainley and Luntley 2005).

> What distinguishes mere craft from profession is the indeterminacy of rules when applied to particular cases. The professional holds knowledge, not only of how – the capacity for skilled performance – but of what and why. The teacher is... capable of explaining why something is done. The teacher is capable of reflection leading to self-knowledge... (Shulman 1987, 13)

The most effective teachers are reflective about their practice (Pedder, James and MacBeath 2005).

To bring student teachers to this level of critical reflection requires more than apprenticeship as a trainee in a school. Higher education (HE) has a significant role to play in educating students to be able to reflect critically and analyse their own practice.

For HE to play this distinctive role in the education of student teachers, tutors in universities must themselves have deep pedagogical knowledge and an ability to analyse and reflect on practice. It can be argued, therefore, that to maintain the critical integrity of pedagogical practice it is essential that research is sustained and developed in institutions that provide teacher education. This is particularly true given that most Initial Teacher Education and Training (ITET) courses now offer master's-level credit, demanding critical analysis of practice and research literature.

However, in the UK research quality has been assessed and rewarded through a process known as the Research Assessment Exercise (RAE). The funding which follows success in the RAE is significant and it is of concern that the process is leading to increased differentiation between research-intensive and teaching-intensive institutions (Pollard 2008).

McIntyre and McIntyre (1999) distinguish between four types of research about teaching and learning:

(1) research aimed at applying knowledge from social sciences to policies and practices for teaching and learning;
(2) educational research aimed at achieving improved understanding of teaching and learning practices, processes and contexts;
(3) research designed to provide direct evidence of effective approaches to teaching and learning;
(4) practitioner research and especially schools as research and learning institutions.

(McIntyre and McIntyre 1999, v)

The funding for the maintenance and development of the first category, so-called basic or pure research, has been safeguarded by the criteria applied by the RAE. The second and third, most often to be found in teacher education institutions has been less well supported and valued as an academic outcome. The distribution of core funding for educational research on the basis of successive RAEs has resulted in many newer universities, which were formerly teacher education institutions, receiving little or no funding to develop and sustain a healthy research infrastructure. One of the consequences of this trend can be seen in the reduction in the number of research papers that focused on pedagogy which were submitted to the RAE in 2008:

> Some more traditional areas were less strongly represented than previously e.g. leadership and management, teacher education, international/comparative education… Other fields continued to be under-represented in relation to their key importance to national education systems e.g. assessment (at all levels), classroom learning and effective teaching in subject disciplines, middle management in schools… (RAE 2008, 2)

The increasing separation, and possible divorce, between teacher education and its research base could inflict profound damage on the quality of teacher professional development. An engagement with research by teacher educators – to enable critical review of existing research and to generate new knowledge – is needed to increase the quality of student learning (Menter, Brisard and Smith 2006; Murray et al. 2009). Teacher-educator-researchers need to have the confidence to operate on all four of the aforementioned levels. A research capacity within teacher education institutions provides the bedrock of a research culture for the sector (Furlong et al. 2006).

In this paper we will focus on the Welsh Education Research Network (WERN), a pilot project to build educational research capacity in Wales. WERN was funded by the Economic and Social Research Council (ESRC) and the Higher Education Funding Council for Wales (HEFCW). We will begin by describing the context in Wales including an overview of the initiatives introduced by WERN, before continuing to examine in greater detail a case study of one WERN inter-institutional collaborative group and its impact on research capacity of the participating researchers and their institutions. We will conclude by discussing the consequences for participating staff, their students and their institutions of research engagement, and reflect on the implications of the findings of this case study for the quality of teacher education.

Capacity building in Wales

Wales has 11 institutions with education or related departments, eight of these provide ITET courses. Education research capacity in Wales has steadily declined over the last two decades, and this trend has been well documented (Furlong and White 2001; Rees and Power 2007; Daugherty and Davies 2008). The results of the 2008 RAE (summarised in Table 1) confirm a continuing downward trajectory. Cardiff University, which had been the sole recipient of core educational research funding in Wales following the 2001 RAE, did not make a submission to the education sub-panel. Education research at Cardiff School of Social Sciences is substantially focused on studies of education and the 'knowledge economy', developing sociological approaches to the analysis of the relationships between education and training systems and the labour market. Consequently, Cardiff, a research-intensive and well-research-funded institution, included its education research within a submission to the sociology sub-panel.

Of the remainder, six institutions made submissions to the education sub-panel. The 2008 RAE adopted a four-way classification of the quality of work in terms of originality, significance and rigour: 4* was judged world-leading; 3* was internationally excellent; 2* was internationally recognised and 1* nationally recognised, with 'unclassified' being a self-explanatory category. Table 1 shows that the majority of institutions in Wales that made a submission to the education sub-panel achieved an overall quality profile that was substantially at the 1* level or unclassified. Bangor and Glamorgan, the exceptions, achieved better but still received overall profiles that indicate the majority of their activity is 2* or below. What is also notable from these results is the low number of research-active staff (37 full-time equivalent academic staff) returned in total for Wales.

Although as a result of judgements made by the education sub-panel some limited funding will find its way to most of the institutions that made a submission, it is very unlikely that this will reverse the trend of increasing differentiation between research-intensive and teaching-intensive institutions in Wales. Moreover, as a result, there remains a danger that educational research into pedagogy may wither and teacher education may become separated from its research base.

It can be argued that the ultimate purpose of educational research is to improve the effectiveness of teaching and learning. Many of the institutions in Wales that have low research capacity, are providers of initial and continuing teacher education, and as a result have high levels of connectedness with educational practice and policy. Academic staff, many of whom have prior professional experience in the classroom, are able to contribute unique insights and practitioner knowledge which can be of

Table 1. Research Assessment Exercise Education sub-panel results for Wales.

Institution	FTE Category A staff submitted**	Percentage of research activity in submission judged to meet the standard				
		4*	3*	2*	1*	Unclassified
Aberystwyth University⁺	No submission made to education sub-panel					
Cardiff University⁺	Submission made to sociology sub-panel					
Bangor University⁺*	4.66	10	20	20	35	15
University of Wales Institute Cardiff⁺*	10.00	0	0	30	50	20
University of Glamorgan	6.75	0	20	35	35	10
Glyndwr University*	5.70	0	5	20	35	40
University of Newport⁺*	1.00	0	0	25	55	20
Swansea Metropolitan University⁺*	8.89	5	10	30	40	15
Swansea University	No submission made to education sub-panel					
Trinity University College⁺*	No submission made to education sub-panel					
Open University in Wales⁺	No submission made to education sub-panel					

Notes: FTE, full-time equivalent; ⁺post-graduate teacher training provider; *initial teacher training provider; **Category A staff have contracts that list research and/or teaching as their primary function.

tremendous value for applied educational research (Davies and Salisbury 2008). However, as capacity shrinks, there are fewer and fewer opportunities for new or second-career researchers, after entering HE, to develop research skills by either formal training or informal 'learning alongside' more experienced peers.

Underlying this general picture of decline, it is possible to identify differences between teacher education institutions with regard to their research tradition and the environment that exists for research. With the exception of Cardiff (which remains a thriving, research-intensive university) there exist only pockets of educational research expertise in some of the other pre-1992 universities.

The post-1992 universities do not for the most part have a history of strong engagement with research but do aspire to build a positive environment for its growth. Although they had not received core funding from successive RAEs some have taken modest steps to build their capacity (Daugherty and Davies 2008).

Nevertheless, despite some institutions following an encouraging trajectory, education research capacity in Wales is not healthy and some might consider it on the 'critical list'. WERN was jointly funded by ESRC and HEFCW to trial methods to arrest the decline and re-build capacity. WERN aims to build research collaboration in order to develop inter-institutional clusters of research expertise which are viable as 'communities of practice' (Lave and Wenger 1991) and have sufficient 'critical mass' to attract funding and in so doing increase future sustainability.

The rationale for WERN rests on a social practices model. There is a sound body of knowledge that supports this position (Davies and Salisbury 2008). This literature (e.g., Eraut and Hirsch 2007) suggests that working alongside more experienced peers can foster and empower the learning of new professional skills.

During its first year (2007–2008) WERN's principal strategy was the provision of bursaries to support groups of colleagues from different institutions to work together to develop and submit a proposal for research funding. WERN funding was allocated by competition and an essential criterion was a mix of skills and expertise within the group that had the potential to mentor and build the capacity of the group members. External evaluation at the conclusion of the initial funding period judged WERN to be successful (Gardner 2008).

ESRC and HEFCW funding was then extended to the end of July 2009. In the second year WERN continued the group bursary scheme but extended its range of collaborative funding initiatives to also include group bursaries for small-scale research projects and launched a Collaborative Fellowship Scheme. The Collaborative Fellowship offered new or mid career researchers the opportunity to develop a specified research skill, by working alongside a mentor who could demonstrate its use in the field. The development and evaluation of WERN during its first year is described in Davies and Salisbury (2009).

One of the bursary groups funded by WERN in its first year called itself the i-ped project and aimed to investigate the affordances of information and communication technology (ICT) for the development of effective pedagogy in mathematics and science classrooms. The term 'affordance' was originally coined by Gibson (1977). Affordances are the 'qualities of systems that can support interactions for an individual to participate in' (Greeno and the Middle School Mathematics Application Project Group 1998, 9) and the concept is often used when analysing the ICT human interface. The experiences of that project are offered here as a case study to illustrate the experiences of participants in the WERN bursary scheme and the extent to which involvement in the i-ped project afforded the development of research capacity and reflection on teacher educator researchers' own practices.

The i-ped project

The i-ped bursary group was a large one and involved 11 staff with a wide variety of research backgrounds from three collaborating universities in Wales and a mentor, from Durham University (see Tanner et al. 2009 for details). The project aimed to develop research capacity in three Welsh universities; Swansea Metropolitan University, University of Wales Institute Cardiff and Trinity College Carmarthen.

The collaborative activities of the group always served two purposes that ran in parallel. The first focus was the development of a research proposal that could gain external research funding. The proposed research would investigate the affordances of ICT for the development of effective dialogical pedagogies in mathematics and science classrooms. The second focus of the collaborative activity was of equal importance and was the development of research skills and theoretical understanding amongst the group through research training and collaborative activity in preparation for submitting a research proposal.

The focus of our research activity

In recent years, schools in England and Wales have invested heavily in ICT resources that might be expected to support the development of interactive pedagogies. In particular, the use of projective technologies such as interactive whiteboards and data-projectors has become common. However research indicates that the impact of such technologies on pedagogy and learning has been, at best, variable. Although projective technologies have features that have the potential to support dialogical pedagogies, classical forms of teacher–student interaction appear to be very resilient. The traditional classroom recitation script of initiation–response–feedback (IRF) (Sinclair and Coultard 1975) dominates in most classrooms. Dialogical pedagogies struggle to gain acceptance alongside established classical approaches which have semi-official status and a didactical infrastructure even when supported by ICT (Smith et al. 2005; Smith, Hardman, and Higgins 2006; Moss et al. 2007).

In contrast to the basic repertoire of classroom interaction, dominated by IRF, dialogical approaches are characterised by a discourse that is collective, reciprocal, supportive, cumulative and purposeful (Alexander 2005). Dialogical pedagogies require more than superficial participation by students; they require teachers to uptake children's ideas, offering the opportunity for students to modify the course of instruction. However, as these processes are complex and ill-defined, they are less frequently encountered in UK classrooms (Nystrand et al. 2003; Tanner et al. 2005).

Four members of the i-ped team had been co-researchers on the Teaching and Learning Research Programme project 'Interactive teaching and ICT' (ITICT), which explored the nature of interactive teaching and the potential mediating influence of ICT tools on the teaching and learning process. The findings of ITICT highlight the limited influence of ICT in improving attainment compared with the effect of dialogic pedagogy and the need for further research into how pedagogical practices may be developed which integrate ICT in support of dialogic teaching (Kennewell et al. 2008).

i-ped aimed to build on the results, insights and research expertise gained in the ITICT project to gain external funding to investigate how ICT can support the development of dialogical pedagogies in mathematics and science. The intended project would explore which affordances of ICT were being integrated into pedagogy and what factors influenced the interaction between ICT and pedagogy in the differing social, cultural and political contexts of Wales and England.

The genesis and rationale underpinning teachers' pedagogies is not directly accessible to researchers. A fundamental aspect of the methodology of the ITICT project was the use of Video Stimulated Reflective Dialogue (VSRD). This involved researchers observing and video-taping lessons. Sections of video, chosen by the teacher, were then used at a later date to stimulate a dialogue between the teacher and researchers about aspects of pedagogy. This proved to be an effective process through which researchers were able to gain insight into the current state of teachers' explicitly stated pedagogical thinking, including any underpinning rationale for their approaches and their reflections on directions for future development. VSRD was planned to be a key aspect of the i-ped project.

WERN's social practices model encouraged the formation of groups with a wide level of expertise in research terms. Some members of the i-ped group were experienced researchers with research and publication records that would be acceptable to funding councils. Other members of the group were highly experienced in teacher education and training and were skilled, knowledgeable and experienced teachers, but were relatively new to research and the production of publications. We refer to these professionals whose academic life follows a previous period in another occupation as *second-career researchers*.

Second-career researchers in teacher education have a heavy teaching load and find it difficult to develop a research and publication track record. Unfortunately, without such a track record, they are unlikely to be successful as named researchers on a bid to a funding council, which would allow them to develop the research skills they require.

The development strategy

i-ped aimed to develop practical research skills and theoretical understanding amongst the group through collaborative activity and training whilst developing a small-scale research proposal.

Rather than developing research knowledge and skills in isolation which may or may not be employed later, the early-career researchers were working alongside more experienced colleagues engaged in the social practices of research, writing bids, designing investigations, discussing theory etc., while exploring a genuine research focus. Although they were inexperienced in some aspects of our work, the second-career researchers brought a wealth of experience in schools and education which they were able to deploy in legitimate and meaningful ways while engaged alongside more experienced researchers in a collaborative project.

However, the relationship was not that of novice and mentor. Team meetings addressed issues of pedagogy and research methodology that were always sufficiently complex to ensure that the knowledge and skills of *all* participants were being extended. Each member of the team brought specific knowledge and expertise to a dialogue that pooled thinking about pedagogical and research issues. i-ped aimed to develop the research expertise of the second-career researchers progressively with a view to being named as research assistants on a proposal that might be made to a research council. Initial meetings focused on the nature of dialogic teaching with ICT, lesson observation and analysis, interviewing and VSRD. The results of the ITICT project were discussed and issues associated with its research strategies were analysed.

Interactive or dialogic teaching is ill-defined in the literature, and the team needed to develop a common understanding of the issues. Video clips of lessons were analysed with a view to developing consistency of judgement when using the theoretical observation framework that had been employed on the ITICT project. Although all members of the team were experienced in analysing lessons with the aim of assessing trainee teachers against the standards required for Qualified Teacher Status (QTS), this was not the stance that we would be taking as researchers. As researchers the team were not aiming to judge teachers against a perceived model of good practice. Rather the intention was to record and analyse the decisions and actions taken by teachers in their own terms, according to their own pedagogical principles.

In parallel with this theoretical activity, the group worked collaboratively on the development of a small-scale proposal to the British Educational Communications and Technology Agency (Becta – a government agency encouraging the effective use of technology) to research the use of VSRD as a staff development tool to develop dialogical teaching approaches using ICT in mathematics and science. In an early meeting, small groups worked on networked laptops to create elements of the proposal. An interactive whiteboard was then used to merge ideas on screen and engage in collaborative refinement of the proposal. Further refinement occurred via e-mail the next day. The process of preparing the proposal was genuinely collaborative and should be seen as an element of capacity building. The Becta proposal was designed with the second-career researchers playing a central role in a project based on VSRD. The aim was to develop their research skills progressively in this area so that the whole team could claim expertise in VSRD in a future ESRC bid. In March 2008 the group learned that the bid to Becta had been successful and the research training and knowledge building that occurred in the remaining formal meetings of the group were infused with a sense of urgency that the team would be using the techniques in the field within a short time.

The next stage in the research training was for each of the second-career researchers to use VSRD as a research tool with their trainee teachers. Lessons by trainees were video-recorded. Videos remained the property of the trainees who took them away to analyse in preparation for a reflective dialogue when the researcher returned. For ethical reasons the VSRD process was deliberately separated from the QTS assessment process. Assessment visits to these trainees were conducted by other staff. The usual ethical guidelines were followed, including gaining voluntary informed consent from trainees, students, schools and parents. The second-career researchers reported back on the outcomes of the reflective dialogue interviews at the next i-ped meeting. The discussion operated on three levels: (1) the impact of VSRD on the professional development of the trainee; (2) the efficacy of VSRD as a research tool; and (3) the research skills that had been developed in the process.

The second-career researchers explored the issues associated with the use of the theoretical framework and the practical problems associated with video recording classroom action, taking contemporaneous research notes and triangulating observations. Issues that had arisen were discussed with the whole team in the next meeting. Video-recorded lesson segments were then analysed by the team using the agreed theoretical framework and judgements were moderated through discussion.

The Becta project

The Becta project aimed to evaluate the efficacy of VSRD as a school-based professional development tool for improving pedagogy in the use of ICT to support dialogic teaching in mathematics and science classrooms. The project utilises digital video to stimulate teachers' thinking about the decisions they were making about their use of ICT and the extent to which it supported the process of dialogic teaching. The resulting reflective dialogue would then be explored as a model of coaching. The research used a mixed-methods action research design with teachers and researchers working collaboratively to develop and evaluate effective dialogic teaching strategies involving ICT in science and mathematics lessons.

The sample

The team drew on their school contacts to identify teachers who interested in developing their use of ICT to support dialogic teaching. Eight teachers from four schools volunteered to join the project.

Table 2. The sample of teachers in the Becta project.

Subject	Key Stage 2 (7–11 years)	Key Stage 3 (11–14 years)
Mathematics	2 teachers	2 teachers
Science	2 teachers	2 teachers

Data collection and analysis

The project began with an initial workshop for all the teachers and researchers teachers and researchers to begin to develop a shared understanding of the nature of dialogical teaching and the aims of the project. Discussions recorded at this meeting also provided baseline data about the teachers' articulated thinking about pedagogy and use of ICT.

Two cycles of action research then followed (see Figure 1). At the start of each cycle, teachers identified an aspect of practice which they wished to develop and nominated a lesson to be video-recorded. Lessons were observed by two researchers (one less and one more experienced) and contemporaneous field notes were taken using a framework for analysis developed in the ITICT project (Kennewell et al. 2008). The more experienced researcher usually operated the camera, leaving the less experienced researcher to take the lead role. The DVD remained the property of the teacher, who took it away to watch and reflect on. Approximately a week later, the teacher came into one of the universities to watch their video in a quiet environment, make notes, select clips and then engage in a reflective dialogue. The teacher controlled the precise focus of the dialogue by selecting the initial clips of video to be discussed. The trajectory and pace of the post-observation dialogue was then largely controlled by the teachers, although the focus remained on the use of ICT to support dialogical teaching.

During the VSRD, a framework of prompts was used to focus the dialogue, rather than a detailed set of questions which might be too extensive to select from during the natural course of discussion (Moyles, Hargreaves and Merry 2003):

- The teacher's reasons for selecting the lesson clips
- Approaches/strategies used in the lesson and their reasons for choosing them
- Approaches considered but not used and the reasons why
- Value of ICT in the lesson or reasons why ICT was not appropriate
- Impact on students' learning
- Impact on the teacher's views of the role of dialogic teaching and ICT

While the second-career researcher managed the dialogue, the experienced researcher observed the VSRD process, and made an audio and video record for later analysis. The first VSRD concluded with the teacher identifying a focus for further exploration or development during the second action research cycle.

At the end of the second cycle, in July 2008, teachers and researchers met as a group to evaluate the project and to reflect collectively on the experience. Part of the day focused on the efficacy of VSRD as a tool for staff development and the conditions that were necessary for it to be most effective. Discussions focused on strategies for working with colleagues in school which would support the sharing and development of effective practice. Data from lesson observations, discussions during the meetings and the transcripts of VSRD were used to identify and analyse:

(1) ICT and dialogic teaching
(2) Change in practice
(3) Effect of the overall process

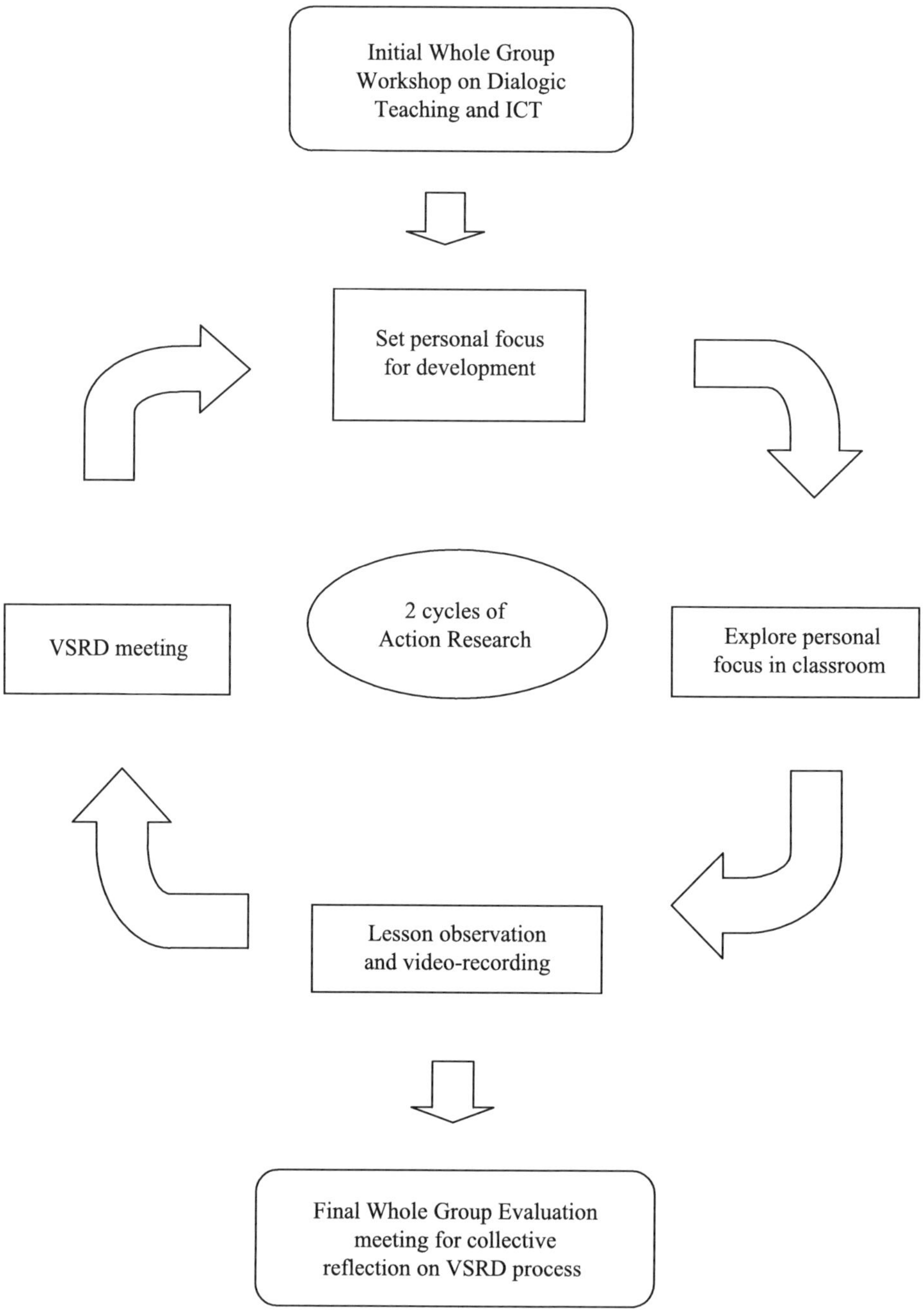

Figure 1. The action research cycles.

Although the fieldwork for the Becta project had been completed at this stage, data analysis had not. The i-ped group met again in September 2008 to discuss:

(1) What had been learned in the Becta project;
(2) Writing plans;
(3) A strategy for developing a bid to ESRC for further funding; and
(4) The impact of involvement in WERN and subsequently Becta on professional development.

The final report for Becta was produced in December 2008. In parallel with this, collaborative papers were prepared for the *Welsh Journal of Education* on the work of the i-ped project and the Becta project (Tanner et al. 2009; S. Jones et al. 2009). All of the team are named as authors on the papers, with the exception of one team member who did not join the Becta project due to pressure of work following promotion to a senior position within their institution.

Impact

The final meetings of i-ped and Becta included sessions in which team members were invited to comment on the impact of their involvement with WERN and subsequently Becta on their professional development. These discussions were wide ranging, but were semi-structured in that they addressed the following issues:

- Knowledge and understanding of:
  - Pedagogy
  - Educational research
- Research skills
- Professional life:
  - Teaching
  - Scholarship

These discussions were recorded through contemporaneous notes and audio-recording. In spring 2009 the i-ped team members were also invited to comment under these headings by email. Non-response was followed up through telephone interviews.

All of the team members were positive about the impact of the projects. The second-career researchers were particularly positive about what they had learned. All of the team commented on the insights they had gained into pedagogy. A second-career researcher with long experience of teaching in HE commented: '[The projects] made me more aware of interactivity and I now tend to analyze this when observing practice in schools and reflecting on my own lecturing style'. The comment that the project had changed their awareness of interactivity in the classroom when observing student teachers was common. Most also claimed to have reflected on their own teaching practices.

Several researchers commented on the new insights they had gained when discussing the interaction between theory and pedagogy: 'I have gained knowledge in terms of research/theory into pedagogy – e.g. interaction scales'. Although the nature of good practice as discussed by inspectors and government strategies was well known. The extent to which such practices were recognised as being soundly based in a theoretical framework had been more variable. The value of shared critical analysis of sections of lessons was appreciated: 'I really valued being able to discuss lesson clips in depth with other researchers to analyse examples of good dialogic teaching and subsequently apply what I had learned to my own teaching'. Although teacher educators observe students teaching on a regular basis, they do not often have the opportunity to analyse discourse moves in depth with fellow academics. The value of being involved in that process was recognised. Although ITET tutors are in school on a regular basis several commented on the advantage of visiting school with a different purpose: 'The "in school" part provided useful insight into how teachers may be interpreting recommendations and materials'. The discrepancy between policy and practice is sometimes wide. Understanding how experienced teachers were interpreting guidelines and making pedagogical decisions was seen as a valuable aspect of engaging in classroom based research.

All the second-career researchers commented on the value of being personally involved in educational research and the new insights they had developed: 'Being actively involved in research like this has opened my eyes to what is involved and the level of critical detachment that a researcher has to achieve'. For most of the second-career researchers, involvement in research was seen as empowering. Although they had become more aware of some of the difficulties involved in conducting effective research, they now felt it was within their capabilities.

The more experienced researchers talked about insights they had gained into the VSRD process and the complexity of analysing classroom interactions:

> I now distinguish much more clearly between video stimulated reflection (VSR) in which the researcher's role is largely to be a neutral facilitator and VSRD in which the aim is create a genuine professional dialogue with both parties contributing to the development of new pedagogical knowledge.

The complex nature of dialogical pedagogy had been analysed in some depth during the project and all the researchers felt that they had developed deeper understanding. The second-career researchers commented about a range of new research skills that they had learned:

> I had the opportunity to conduct interviews, write field notes, record sessions on video, analyze transcripts, and contribute to group reflection and working meetings.

> I really valued the technique of sitting down with my co-researcher immediately after a school visit to compare notes and analyse the interactions we had observed in the classroom.

The value of gaining research skills in a social context, whilst collaborating on a research project was recognised. All the team commented on the value of being able to discuss complex issues with co-researchers. The more experienced researchers also found this valuable: 'I found the conversations with other researchers particularly useful in terms of clarifying my own understanding of situations'. One second-career researcher commented on the value of the mixture of experience: 'It was a good experience to work with alongside a mix of experienced and novice researchers. I felt like I wasn't the only new kid on the block and that my opinion counted'. All the second-career researchers commented on the impact that the project had had on their professional lives. All the team had reflected on the ways that they managed discussions in university seminars and had drawn parallels with the deeper understandings they had developed about the nature of dialogue:

> Analysing how X managed a discussion in the classroom has made me reflect on my own teaching and I now try to use some of those techniques when I manage discussions in University.

> It has made me much more critically reflective about my own practice and to focus much more closely on what I hope to achieve in discussions.
>
> I used VSRD for peer observation as a part of my staff development. I have learned a lot about my own teaching and it has helped me to become much more reflective about my own practice.

The impact of the projects can be seen in the continuing professional development of some of the second-career researchers. Research is continuing beyond the end of the project at a range of levels. One second-career researcher has registered for a PhD and another has registered for a research master's degree. Both valued the skills they had learned in the projects and the confidence they had gained. Another was conducting unfunded research into an area of personal interest in her spare time. Involvement with WERN was continuing:

> I have my own small project award and am researching in Foundation Phase.
>
> I have a WERN collaborative research fellowship, including writing a research report.
>
> I have presented aspects of the research at Research Day at University, with teachers from a participating primary school.

Senior managers regard the involvement of their staff in the projects very positively. One senior manager commented:

> From my point of view, I've certainly gained the impression that both [second-career researchers] have gained a great deal in relation to all the areas you identify.
>
> I think their involvement with the projects has also had a very positive effect on some others within the School of ITET who have been encouraged to think that maybe they should also be thinking in terms of getting involved / started with a research project of their own.

Another said:

> I can see a real difference in X. They are more confident in their role as an academic and are keen to be involved in further research. It's as if being involved in projects like this added credibility to their claims about their understanding of classroom processes as an ITET tutor.
>
> They are more reflective about their own teaching. Having reflected critically on the pedagogical practices of experienced teachers, they seem more able to reflect critically on their own practice.

The only negative comments made by members of the team related to the shortage of time available to engage with writing up the research: 'I would have liked to follow up on the process of writing papers/conference abstracts etc.'; 'I just wish I had more time to have worked on this project'.

Discussion

Learning to teach is far more than simply acquiring a set of skills and routines of performance. In order to make effective judgements in the moment during the fast flow of lessons, the most effective teachers rely on a deep understanding of pedagogy built up through reflection on practice and critical analysis of praxis. All the ITET tutors involved in these projects developed a deeper understanding of pedagogy through their own reflection and critical analysis of praxis during the research process. Furthermore, they were able to identify ways in which this would impact on their own professional practice as ITET tutors.

To build a culture of reflective practice, research must be an essential part of teacher professional development from the outset. This case study would suggest that teacher educators who are familiar with, and engaged with, research are better able to model the skills and practices of empirical enquiry to their students who can then integrate them into their emerging professional practices.

The accounts of group members comment on the value of this research, based around peer observation, for reflecting on their own practice. In terms of the development of their professional role, their responses can be grouped into three key ways in which being research active has influenced their teacher-education practice. First, it involved a thorough and critical analysis of the literature and later the data gathered, which strengthened their knowledge of the field. Increased knowledge of relevant scholarship has the potential to impact positively on the quality of teaching, and some of the group talked about project reading finding their way into their teaching.

Second, it developed their capacity to understand and undertake research. This provides new skills and confidence to maintain research activity as part of professional life, perhaps by continuing as part of a collaborative research team or engaging in study for a doctorate. However improved knowledge of research skills also has had a direct impact on the quality of the student experience by enhancing the delivery of research modules and the supervision of student research activity.

Third, and perhaps most importantly, becoming a researcher developed their critical awareness and evaluative skills. Becoming critical challenges the teacher-educator to re-assess preconceptions, question accepted orthodoxies, re-evaluate existing theories and develop and test new hypotheses. Integrating these perspectives into professional practice provides a model for students that will encourage the students in turn to become reflective practitioners.

The case study also illustrates some of the pressures, documented in the literature (for example, Murray 2007), that hinder teacher-educators as they struggle to become, and remain, research active. Most pressing is the lack of time because research may not be an institutional priority, and there are a mass of other teaching, managerial and bureaucratic demands which require more urgent response. Even when funding is provided, as was the case with the WERN bursary, the institution, can sometimes lack the flexibility and infrastructure that might be found in a research orientated institution and which would enable best use to be made of this support. The evaluation of the progress of WERN has identified that growth in capacity amongst individual researchers is unlikely to be sustained without corresponding institutional development (Davies and Salisbury 2008). In part this is about strategic and managerial priorities, but it is also about changing the interests and motivations of staff. As one institutional manager commented:

> 'Looking over the shoulder' of those doing research stimulates interest. There is a slow creep of people seeing other people involved, getting time off for research, heads have been turning. We have been changing the culture that before people weren't being released, slowly things are changing.

In this case the actions of individual researchers are influencing colleagues, and so are helping to build a community and an institutional culture where research is important and valued.

The research group that has been described here came about as a result of a small investment by WERN, which then realised additional funding from Becta. It has developed the research skills of all its members, all of whom continue to be research active. Two early-career researchers, as a result of working in this collaborative group have gone on to attract further research funding from WERN. One has embarked on a doctorate and another is progressing on a master of research degree. Members of the team continue to collaborate on different projects as appropriate – the network of potential collaborators continues to grow.

All the institutions involved have supported their staff, albeit within the constraints of their existing research infrastructure. Senior and middle management have provided encouragement and have recognised the importance of staff engaging actively with research. The institutions have benefited not only from the enhanced knowledge and skills that research activity has created but from the contribution that is made to the development of a research culture that underpins the scholarly activities of a university community.

Conclusion

WERN's mission is to develop educational research capacity in Wales. Why, one could ask, would it be a significant loss if educational research were to disappear from teacher education institutions? Although only based on data from one case study, this paper offers some tentative ripostes to such a question by outlining how the experience of research activity has changed the practices of one group of teacher-educators. It also provides support for those who argue that there is a need for research capacity in teacher education in its own right as well as part of general capacity building in education (M. Jones et al. 2009).

The results of the 2008 RAE in Wales can be viewed in two ways. The most obvious interpretation is that capacity continues its downward trajectory, and that Welsh educational research is in terminal decline. However, there is a small hope in the core funding that will now be provided to five institutions that had not previously received funding in the 2001 RAE. Although the monies in themselves are not sufficiently large to make a significant difference at the national level, they will act as an incentive to individual institutions to continue to invest in research. The evidence presented in the case study also provides grounds for encouragement to teaching-intensive institutions to develop the research activity of their staff. We have shown that engaging in research can be a powerful tool for the professional development of teacher-educators; therefore research capacity building is an important priority for all who wish to maintain and develop the high quality of education in Wales.

References

Ainley, J., and M. Luntley. 2005. The role of attention in classroom practice: Developing methodology. Proceedings of the 28th annual conference of the Mathematics Education Research Group of Australasia, 7–9 July, in Melbourne. MERGA. http://www.merga.net.au/ documents/RP22005.pdf

Alexander, R. 2005. *Towards dialogic teaching: rethinking classroom talk.* York, UK: Dialogos.

Daugherty, R., and S.M.B. Davies. 2008. Capacity and quality in education research in Wales. Paper presented at the Strategic Forum for Research in Education, 16–17 October, in Harrogate, UK.

Davies, S.M.B., and J. Salisbury. 2008 Researching and learning together: Inter-institutional collaboration as a means of capacity building. Keynote symposium paper presented at the Annual Conference of the British Education Research Association, 3–6 September, at Heriot Watt University, Edinburgh.

Davies, S.M.B., and J. Salisbury. Forthcoming. Building educational research capacity through inter-institutional collaboration: An evaluation of the first year of the Welsh Education Research Network (WERN). *Welsh Journal of Education* 15: 78–94.

Eraut, M., and W. Hirsch. 2007. *The significance of workplace learning for individuals, groups and organisations. Monograph 6.* Oxford, UK: SKOPE.

Furlong, J., H. Hagger, C. Butcher, and J. Howson. 2006. *Review of initial teacher training provision in Wales. A report to the Welsh Assembly Government.* Oxford, UK: University of Oxford, Department of Educational Studies.

Furlong, J., and P. White. 2001. *Educational research capacity in Wales: A review.* Cardiff, UK: Cardiff University School of Social Sciences.

Gardner, J. 2008. *Welsh education research network: An evaluation.* Belfast, NI: Queens University.

Gibson, J.J. 1977. The theory of affordances. In *Perceiving acting and knowing: Toward an ecological psychology,* ed. R. Shaw and J. Bransford, 67–82. Hillsdale, NJ: Erlbaum.

Greeno, J., and the Middle School Mathematics Application Project Group. 1998. The situativity of knowing, learning and research. *American Psychologist* 53: 5–26.

Jones, M., P. Mahony, O. McNamara, I. Menter, J. Murray, and G. Stanley. 2009. The Teacher Education Research Network (TERN): Building research capacity in the north west region of England. http://www.tlrp.org/tern/docs/Project_Overview.doc

Jones, S., H. Tanner, S. Kennewell, J. Parkinson, H. Denny, C. Anthony, G. Beauchamp, B. Jones, H. Lewis and A. Loughran. 2009. Using video stimulated reflective dialogue to support the development of ICT based pedagogy in mathematics and science. *The Welsh Journal of Education* 15: 63–77.

Kennewell, S., H. Tanner, S. Jones, and G. Beauchamp. 2008. Analysing the use of interactive technology to implement interactive teaching. *Journal of Computer Assisted Learning* 24, no 1: 61–73.

Lave, J., and E. Wenger. 1991. *Situated learning: Legitimate peripheral participation.* Cambridge, UK: Cambridge University Press.

McIntyre, D., and A. McIntyre. 1999. *ESRC teaching and learning programme: Capacity for research into teaching and learning. Final report.* Cambridge, UK: University of Cambridge School of Education.

Menter, I., E. Brisard, and I. Smith. 2006. *Convergence or divergence? Initial teacher education in Scotland and England.* Edinburgh, UK: Dunedin Academic Press.

Moss, G., C. Jewitt, R. Levaaic, V. Armstrong, A. Cardini, and F. Castle. 2007. *The interactive whiteboards, pedagogy and pupil performance evaluation: An evaluation of the schools whiteboard expansion (SWE) project: London challenge.* London: Institute of Education.

Moyles, J., L. Hargreaves, and R. Merry. 2003. Digging even deeper into meanings. In *Interactive teaching in the primary school: Digging deeper into meanings,* ed. J. Moyles, L.

Hargreaves, R. Merry, F. Paterson, and V. Esarte-Sarries, 171–91. Maidenhead, UK: Open University Press.

Murray, J. 2007. Countering insularity in teacher education: Academic work on pre-service courses in nursing, social work and teacher education. *Journal of Education for Teaching* 33, no 3: 271–91.

Murray, J., A. Campbell, I. Hextall, M. Hulme, M. Jones, P. Mahony, I. Menter, R. Proctor, and K. Wall. 2009. Research and teacher education in the UK: Building capacity. *Teaching and Teacher Education* 25: 944–50.

Nystrand. M., L.L. Wu, A. Gamoran, S. Zeiser and D.A. Long. 2003. Questions in time: Investigating the structure and dynamics of unfolding classroom discourse. *Discourse Processes* 35, no 2: 135–98.

Pedder, D., M. James, and J. MacBeath. 2005. How teachers value and practise professional learning. *Research Papers in Education* 20, no 3: 209–43.

Pollard, A. 2008. Towards new strategic initiatives for research capacity in education: A discussion paper. *Building Research Capacity* 13: 1–5.

Rees, G., and S. Power. 2007. Educational research and the restructuring of the state: The impacts of parliamentary devolution in Wales. *European Educational Research Journal* 6, no. 1: 87–99.

Research Assessment Exercise. 2008. Sub-panel 45 education subject overview report. RAE. http://www.rae.ac.uk/pubs/2009/ov/

Shulman, L.S. 1987. Knowledge and teaching: foundations of the new reform. *Harvard Educational Review* 57, no. 1: 1–22.

Sinclair, J., and M. Coultard. 1975. *Towards an analysis of discourse.* Oxford, UK: Oxford University Press.

Smith, F., F. Hardman, and S. Higgins. 2006. The impact of interactive whiteboards on teacher-pupil interaction in the national literacy and numeracy strategies. *British Educational Research Journal* 32, no. 3: 443–57.

Smith, H., S. Higgins, K. Wall, and J. Miller. 2005. Interactive whiteboards: Boon or bandwagon? A critical review of the literature. *Journal of Computer Assisted Learning* 21: 91–101.

Tanner, H., S. Jones, S. Kennewell, and G. Beauchamp. 2005. Interactive whiteboards and pedagogies of whole class teaching. Paper presented at MERGA 28, Mathematics Education Research Group of Australasia Conference, July , in Melbourne, Australia. http://www.merga.net.au/documents/RP832005.pdf.

Tanner, H., S. Jones, S. Kennewell, J. Parkinson, H. Denny, C. Anthony, G. Beauchamp, et al. 2009. An investigation of the affordances of ICT for the development of effective pedagogy in mathematics and science classrooms – the i-ped project. *The Welsh Journal of Education* 15: 136–42.

Capacity = expertise × motivation × opportunities: factors in capacity building in teacher education in England

Jean Murray[a], Marion Jones[b], Olwen McNamara[c] and Grant Stanley[b]

[a]Cass School of Education, University of East London, London, UK; [b]Liverpool John Moores University, Liverpool, UK; [c]University of Manchester, Manchester, UK

This article offers an initial account of the Teacher Education Research Network (TERN), a pilot education research capacity building project funded by the ESRC and designed to test a 'social practices' model for building an educational research infrastructure across England. The TERN project is still running at the time of writing, so it is not yet possible to offer a full evaluation or a theorised analysis of the project. Setting the initiative within the regional context of teacher education in the North West of England, the article describes elements of the project and begins to explore their significance, drawing on early evaluation data. The article adapts Charles Desforges' equation of research capacity building as 'Capacity = expertise × motivation × opportunities' as a frame for this exploration.

Introduction and context

This article offers an initial account of the work of the Teacher Education Research Network (TERN), one of two research capacity building projects in education funded by the Economic and Social Research Council (ESRC) in the academic year 2008/09 to test potential models for building an infrastructure on a larger scale across England. The main aims of TERN are to pilot a strong and sustainable collaborative network of universities in the North West of England for building capacity at institutional and individual levels through an inter-institutional research development programme.

The model of professional learning deployed for the project is based primarily on an 'embedded social practices' principle (Baron 2005) for developing research capacity. The project draws on aspects of both the Applied Educational Research Scheme (AERS) in Scotland and the Welsh Educational Research Network (WERN). The model emphasises situated cognition, stressing the importance for informal professional learning through researchers engaging collaboratively in aspects of the research process (Rees et al. 2007, 776). The TERN project in some ways presents a hybrid version of the social practices model in that it also includes a limited amount of direct pedagogical provision. The intention has been to embed this latter element in the field of teacher education and its research, thereby aiming to avoid the abstraction of 'research methods from the theoretical and philosophical traditions within which they are located, ...[and] from the social context of actual research practice' (Rees et al.

2007, 765). In this respect, TERN shares limited similarities of approach with the first phase of the Teaching and Learning Research Project's (TLRP) research capacity building work and the development of pedagogical resources within the AERS.

Education research as a priority area for capacity building was flagged up in the ESRC's demographic review of the social sciences (ESRC 2006). This review identified a number of ways in which education was significantly different from other social sciences, including the ageing profile of its staff and the low proportion of academics that held doctoral qualifications and/or were designated 'research active'. Teacher education research is 'nested inside of, but also braided with' the generic field of education research (Cochran-Smith and Demers 2008, 1009). Within educational research, teacher education research is an important sub-field (Cochran-Smith and Demers, 2008), albeit 'young', underdeveloped, informed by many different disciplines and subject to rapid policy changes (Zeichner 1999; cited in Cochran-Smith and Zeichner 2006, 755). In the UK much teacher education research is generated by those who are also the educators and managers in the teacher education communities (Furlong 2007; Menter et al. forthcoming). An analysis of UK teacher education research published in key journals between 2000 and 2008 (see Teacher Education Group (TEG) mapping, www.tlrp.org/teg; Murray et al. 2008) indicates that many of the outputs are small-scale, qualitative and practice-based; many might be classified as 'bootstrap research', in which 'researchers take opportunities for research where they find them' (Richardson 2007). As Menter et al. (forthcoming) identify, such factors, together with 'the high number of single studies and the paucity of large-scale, longitudinal studies reduce the potential cumulative and developmental impact of research on and for teacher education in the UK'. In the USA a lack of high quality teacher education research, which is methodologically strong, grounded in relevant theory and built on the foundations of previous research (see Shulman's [1999, 162] definition of 'generativity') has been noted (Cochran-Smith and Zeichner 2006; Richardson 2007). Reflecting these areas of concern from a UK context, the *Subject Overview Report for Education,* which summarised the state of educational research after the last national audit (Research Assessment Exercise [RAE] 2008) singled out teacher education research across the four nations as one of the 'more traditional areas [which] were less strongly represented than previously' (Higher Education and Research Opportunities [HERO] 2008, 12).

In terms of a potential contribution to general efforts to build research capacity building in educational research, however, the importance of 'teacher education' cannot be overestimated. Analyses of the results of the RAE of 2008 (Furlong 2009; Gilroy and McNamara 2009) highlight the considerable and largely untapped potential for teacher educators to contribute to the overall research capacity building needed in education (ESRC 2006). Furlong (2009) estimates that 25% of the universities offering pre-service courses in England did not enter the RAE 2008 at all, and well over a half of the academics working in education departments which did enter, were not 'returned' as active researchers (most of the academics working in education departments are employed as teacher educators, teaching on programmes of pre-service teacher education and continuing professional development for serving teachers). Even after acknowledging the complexity of factors, which might inhibit an institution or an individual from entering the RAE, these figures indicate that research capacity building to increase the volume and quality of research activity in teacher education has a largely unrealised contribution to make to the broad field of education research.

This untapped potential is also significant given the strong communal motivations of a substantial number of teacher educators to engage in research, particularly into aspects of teaching and learning (McIntyre and McIntyre 1999) and their personal practice. These high levels of motivation may also be inferred from analyses of academic engagement in teacher education research (see TEG mapping, www.tlrp.org/teg). One specific example of these levels of motivation is that, in terms of submissions to the British Educational Research Association (BERA) Annual Conference, the Teacher Education Special Interest Group (SIG) has, since its inception in 2005, had the biggest volume of abstracts submitted across all the SIGs. In 2006, for example, Teacher Education had nearly 100 papers submitted, compared with an average of 25 for the other SIGs; in 2008 133 papers were submitted (BERA 2006, 2008).

Why then is teacher education research currently 'punching below its weight'? Existing research (see, *inter alia*, Furlong 2007; Maguire 2000; Murray 2007; Sikes 2006) has identified that a multiplicity of demands often cause tensions for teacher educators, sometimes to the extent of affecting the quality of their practices as academics, or threatening the sustainability of their fields in higher education. This is particularly true for the teacher education workforce in England which has been defined as existing in a 'national framework of accountability' (Furlong et al. 2000, 15) and a 'culture of compliance' (Menter et al. 2006, 50). Pre-service teacher education has also been under sustained pressures from on-going 'reforms' since 1984 (Furlong et al. 2000; Furlong 2005).

The pressures on the teacher education workforce have been reported to include:

(1) the difficulty of attracting suitably qualified staff with Qualified Teacher Status (QTS) from school into higher education because of the relative pay differentials;
(2) the age demographic, accentuated by high proportions of education staff entering higher education following a career switch, profiling over 55% of the current higher education education workforce over the age of 50 and 35% over 55;
(3) the heavy teaching workload and associated accountability and bureaucracy;
(4) the challenge of making the transition between school and higher education cultures, particularly in respect of the requirement to engage in research and scholarly activity; and
(5) the significant reduction in the capacity for research in education overall, which has created a schism in many institutions between teaching and research (McNamara, Brundrett and Webb 2008).

Of particular concern for teacher education, as noted by Gilroy and McNamara (2009) earlier in this issue, is the bifurcation of 'research' and 'teaching', demonstrated in some universities by separate career paths, and in all institutions by a growing disconnect, evident nationally and certainly in the North West region, between research intensive institutions' education departments (many of whom are in receipt of core research funding), and the teaching-intensive universities' education departments which educate the majority of new and serving teachers (with the single exception of Manchester Metropolitan University, all the rest of the post-1992 institutions were not in receipt of any core research funding between 2001 and 2008, and not all pre-1992 university education departments received funding during this period). Dadds and

Kynch (2003) estimated that, as result of this funding policy, 80% of student teachers in 2003 were being educated in institutions without core research funding. The threat of disconnection between research and teaching is particularly significant given the shift in strategic funding towards master's-level study for the teaching profession in England. Many one-year Post Graduate Certificate in Education courses now include elements of master's-level work and the new M-level entry qualification, being piloted in the North West in 2009/10 is to be an entitlement for all newly qualified teachers. The demands which teaching this master's-level work will make on the research skills of the current teacher education workforce are of great concern.

The context chosen for the implementation of the TERN project was the North West – one of the nine English Government Office Regions – which possesses important geographical, political and institutional features with high relevance for testing the potential of such a collaborative project. The region has interesting geographic contrasts: third largest in England in terms of population and sixth in terms of size, it is long and narrow ranging from rural and mountainous Cumbria in the north to the two sprawling urban complexes of Greater Manchester and Merseyside in the south. Currently the region is home to seven universities involved in pre-service teacher education courses for the school sector. All are participating in the project. Their institutional profiles are broadly representative of the range of university settings within which teacher education provision takes place in England. These profiles range from research-intensive pre-1992 universities[1] (Manchester, which is a member of the elite Russell Group of 'old' universities), post-1992 universities (Liverpool John Moores and Manchester Metropolitan, both with origins as polytechnics) and post-2000 universities (Chester, Cumbria, Edge Hill and Hope). With the exception of Manchester, all the universities can be classified as 'teaching-intensive', although Manchester Metropolitan has a strong research base through its Education and Social Research Institute (ESRI).

The North West has a leading role in the pre-service education of teachers in England; an annual allocation of 6000 students makes it the largest region for teacher education outside London. In addition, the teacher education universities have a long history of working together at a strategic level. In terms of education research, however, the region's performance, as measured by numbers of active researchers entered into the RAE has been deeply disappointing. In the 2001 RAE the North West was the third smallest Government Office Region; London and the Midlands accounted for 45% of all educational researchers (Lawn and Furlong 2007). These two factors of heavy institutional and regional investment in teacher education and low levels of research achievements may not be unconnected. In the last decade only two of the original eight universities involved in teacher education in the North West have received sustained core funding for research (Manchester and Manchester Metropolitan), and one research-intensive university (Liverpool) has closed its education department.

The TERN project is still continuing at the time of writing. It is therefore not yet possible to evaluate its impact fully or to offer a theorised account of the initiative, which like many research capacity building endeavours is multi-layered and complex (Erixon Arreman 2008; Pollard 2008; Rees et al. 2007), involving individual, collective, institutional and national interests. In this paper, however, we describe elements of the project and begin to explore their possible significance drawing on early evaluation data. We adapt as a frame for this exploration Charles Desforges' equation for research capacity building as 'Capacity = expertise × motivation × opportunities' (cited in Davies and Salisbury 2008, 9; McIntyre and McIntyre 1999).

We argue for three essential starting points in the design and implementation of research capacity building initiatives. First, providing the opportunities for early- and mid-career researchers to develop their expertise by acquiring new skills, knowledge and understandings of research (see, *inter alia*, Dyson and Desforges 2002; McIntyre and McIntyre 1999; Pollard 2007); second, considering the sense of motivation and agency of the individual researcher, and third, taking into account the socio-cultural contexts for research and scholarship within the university departments of education where the teacher education researchers work (Rees et al. 2007, 776).

The data on which this paper draws include an initial (baseline) mapping of the participants' expertise, baseline interviews with each of the Institutional Research Leaders in the seven universities, the monitoring of participation in face-to-face events, initial analyses of the scale and nature of engagement in the online activities, and paper-based and online evaluations by the participants of the various events and stages in the project, as it has been implemented to date.

Expertise and motivation within the project: starting points

At the start of the project each of the seven universities was asked to nominate six 'mid- or early-career researchers' who were academics involved in teacher education to join the development programme, together with at least one experienced researcher. The aim was to form a number of research groups, including researchers at different career stages and different universities, to work with the support of at least one of the experienced researchers as mentor. During the course of the project, in addition to participating in activities across the network as a whole, each group aimed to develop a research design, which could become a bid to go forward to an external funding body.

Analysis of project data shows that the terms 'early- and mid-career researchers', often used to describe the various stages of academic career trajectories in a range of disciplines (ESRC 2006; Fowler and Procter 2008), were not useful in selecting and describing the participants in this project. This was, in part, because of their varied and diverse career profiles (see later). These profiles led to participants' self-identification as teacher educators, lecturers or teachers rather than researchers. Also significant was the proportion of people without doctoral qualifications, who had nevertheless been involved in significant practitioner or pedagogical research activity. The term 'research fellow' was therefore used to describe all participants, regardless of formal qualifications and/or experience as researchers.

Informal guidance to the universities on the selection of research fellows requested the involvement of individuals who had previous experience of educational research, were 'research aspirant' and involved in teacher education. It was also suggested that the contribution, which individuals could make to strengthening institutional research cultures might well be a significant factor in the selection process. Individual participation in the project was, however, strictly voluntary and grounded in robust ethical protocols.

In order to garner some basic biographical information and establish a baseline of the research fellows' level of confidence, expertise, experience in research, a mapping exercise was conducted through a questionnaire sent out to all participants at the beginning of the project and completed electronically. Analysis of data from the 44 research fellows (30 women and 14 men) that embarked on the project revealed that 76% were over the age of 40, and that the median age band was 40–49 years. Adhering to patterns typical for teacher educators in England (where QTS and experience of teaching in schools or colleges are usually prerequisites for working in teacher education), all the research fellows except one had teaching experience in the elementary, secondary or further education sectors prior to entering higher education. Nearly 60% had more than 10 years' experience of teaching in these sectors, with many holding posts as senior and middle managers, prior to entering higher education.

Fifty-seven percent of all TERN Fellows had made the transition into higher education in the last 10 years, with 23% of those having five or less years of experience. Thirty-six percent had between 10 and 20 years' experience; only a small proportion (7%) had spent 20 years or more in higher education. Thirty-seven percent of research fellows held doctorates (PhDs or the taught doctorate qualification, the EdD), which most had gained through part-time study while working in higher education. This figure is above the 25% national average for education (ESRC 2006). All of the remaining research fellows held master's degrees or undergraduate degrees plus a teaching qualification. Of the 25 participants with master's degrees, 18 were currently enrolled on a doctoral programme. Most of the group (70%) defined their expertise as 'qualitative research', with questionnaires and interviews identified as the most common data collection methods used in previous research.

The motivations of the research fellows for becoming involved in the project were varied, as might be expected. Across the whole data set there are recurring emphases on the development of relevant knowledge and skills. Research fellows also mentioned gaining confidence and developing their research careers. For some, participation had a defined purpose around specific aspects of practice as researchers, for example, creating research bids, writing for academic journals and presenting at conferences. All the following quotations come from the original mapping exercise, which asked why people wanted to join the project and how they hoped to benefit from it individually:

> I hope that my participation will support and enhance my doctoral studies, develop my skills further.
>
> I hope to develop my confidence as a researcher.
>
> [Become] energised, skilled and confident in research practice.
>
> Absorb the expertise of others. Deep critical engagement in the debates.
>
> Support career development in educational research.
>
> I feel that it would support me in providing a sharper focus on my research portfolio, something which tends to be marginalised as things stand.
>
> To gain knowledge of other research techniques and to develop research networks that are capable of bidding for ESRC type projects.

Many respondents emphasised the importance and value, which they placed on the collaborative aspects of the group work within the project. In some cases this was seen as creating valuable regional links with colleagues in neighbouring institutions; in other cases the benefits of networking were related to participation in the wider academic community and/or seen as a way of overcoming isolation:

> Establish cooperative and supportive networks with colleagues form (sic) other institutions and who are engaged in different working practices, with a view to the sustainability of research colleague relationships.
>
> The opportunity to network with other professionals engaged in researching teacher education.
>
> Develop a research network. Collaborative research with other institutions in my field of study.
>
> I normally have to work alone in my subject area and my EdD thesis will not involve working with other lecturers so I look forward to working as part of a research team and hearing the ideas of others.
>
> Engaged in the wider academic community (share knowledge experience, reviewing).

There are 10 research mentors involved in TERN – three from the research-intensive University of Manchester, two from the ESRI at Manchester Metropolitan University and five from the 'pockets of research excellence' in the other North West universities. From the beginning of the project these mentors were seen as central to its success. At the planning stage this aspect of the work was envisaged to draw on relevant characteristics from the TLRP's Meeting of Minds Fellowship scheme (see http://www.tlrp.org/capacity/rm/fellowships.html). But whereas these Fellowships are based on a one-to-one model of mentoring, the TERN project envisages adapting mentoring to working with small groups (a 'one-to-some' or 'one-to-many' model).

Each research group worked on developing well-structured research designs to address communally defined research questions with high relevance to teacher education. The process of identifying potential themes around which research groups could be formed proved a challenging undertaking, and could best be described as iterative and democratic in intent at least. Aiming to make this process successful was clearly of key importance in mobilising individual and institutional expertise and initial motivations to secure the year-long commitments to the project.

The overall aim of the process (see Table 1) was to enable participants to feel some sense of ownership at each stage of the process and to retain feelings of commitment and motivation. It began with the identification of tentative themes. These subsequently underwent further refinement and crystallisation during the process of creating the research groups. A further priority in the process was to ensure that individual expertise and motivations could be well aligned with the identified nationally and regionally relevant themes for teacher education research. A sensitive approach was adopted in managing existing allegiances, taking into account individual preferences and expertise, mentors' expertise and, where relevant, institutional priorities.

Some fine tuning of group membership occurred in response to research fellows' and mentors' preferences and needs as research themes began to develop clearer foci. This happened largely between Workshops 1 and 2. Some re-alignment was also necessary to accommodate individual expertise; a very small number of re-alignments were also made to accommodate challenging inter-personal dynamics within groups. Judgements about the extent to which this negotiated process was or was not successful in aligning individual and institutional expertise and motivations with the emerging research themes must await the results of the final evaluation. But it certainly resulted in groups of unequal size, and in some cases, with an uneven spread of types of researcher expertise and numbers of universities involved. As we indicate later, there are already indications that these final allocations of individuals to groups may

Table 1. The process of aligning research themes, fellows and mentors.

Event	Date	Focus	Participation
Pre-launch	Oct 2008	Analysis of areas of research fellows' research interests and expertise	Core team
Launch event	Nov 08	Discussion groups to identify project's research themes, of national and regional relevance to teacher education	All research fellows and mentors
Mentor meeting	Nov 2008	Distillation of research themes and interests to give first iteration of research groups and mapping of mentor expertise	Core team and mentors
Email and telephone discussions	Dec 2008	Negotiation of first (and second) iteration(s) of research groups with research fellows	Core team and research fellows, with guidance from mentors
Workshop 1	Jan 2009	First face-to-face meeting of research fellows and mentors in their respective research groups	All research fellows and mentors

well have had distinct influences on the differentiated individual and group learning outcomes across the project.

Opportunities for learning within the project

Providing a detailed account of the development and final form of the project is not the focus of this article, but in the following section we briefly sketch the opportunities which the project aimed to provide for the participants. As noted previously, the broad structures and content for the professional learning programme, which formed the backbone of the TERN project, were determined by the findings of previous 'social practices' initiatives on developing institutional and individual research expertise. But in designing the precise structures and contents of the TERN programme the following elements were used to fine tune provision: the regional context for teacher education; the socio-cultural contexts for research and scholarship within the university departments of education where the research fellows work; the participants' previous experiences, expertise and motivations as educational researchers; and previous research on teacher educators' professional learning, particularly in relation to managing the development of research and scholarship (Murray 2008) and tensions in the teaching-scholarship nexus (Deem and Lucas 2007; Maguire 2000; Nixon 1996; Sikes 2006).

Again, a detailed account of how these elements shaped the design of the project is not our aim here, but indicative influences are briefly sketched. Previous research indicating the pressures on teacher educators' time and opportunities to research (Maguire 2000; Sikes 2006; Furlong 2007) led to the high degree of structure provided in the programme, particularly the identification and protection of designated days for the face-to-face meetings. In a further attempt to protect time for the project, all institutions and individuals were asked to make commitments at the beginning of the project to facilitating research fellows' and mentors' attendance at all the workshops, wherever possible. Findings about the current types of teacher education research in the UK (predominantly qualitative, small-scale and lacking a true sense of generativity, see earlier; Furlong 2009; Menter et al. forthcoming; Murray et al. 2009), combined with the analysis of research fellows' developmental needs as researchers, determined the focus of the direct pedagogical inputs at each event. Work on how the values and missions of teacher educators affect individual and communal development as researchers (Boyd et al. 2005; Harrison and McKeon 2008; Murray 2007; Murray and Mahony 2009) influenced the democratic and grounded process, described previously, of deciding on research themes. One of the main questions which arose from the mapping of the existing knowledge, expertise and motivations within the project was how the design and implementation of the research development programme could offer enhanced learning opportunities to research fellows with differing levels of research expertise and professional experience and varying motivations for engaging in the project. A further question was around how these variations could be best deployed within the small research groups in order to maximise professional learning for all.

The resulting research development programme aims to strengthen individual and communal expertise. Its specific objectives are: to provide well-focused research training and mentoring to early- and mid-career researchers; to explore the theoretical, methodological and substantive issues involved in generating high-quality teacher education research; and to identify and address an under-researched issue, which has contemporary relevance and potential to inform practice in teacher education. As indicated previously, the programme also aims to ensure purposeful dissemination and use of the TLRP research capacity building resources, particularly the methodological resources and the mapping of TEG.

Figure 1 shows the final design of the research development programme, which was central to the project. Five face-to-face events (workshops) were organised, the first four of which had a direct pedagogical input on a theoretical, substantive or methodological aspect of teacher education research, identified as relevant to the needs of the participants through the baseline mapping (see Table 2). A launch event was utilised to begin the process of negotiating the research themes and a final event (Workshop 5) will be used for dissemination of the work to date. In addition to the five central workshops, two colloquia, funded by ESCalate, were organised to supplement the basic development programme. The latter enabled the chosen theoretical, substantive or methodological emphases to be revisited in more depth.

Table 2. Direct pedagogical inputs at each workshop.

Date	TERN workshop/event
5 November 08	Launch: *Identifying potential themes for research in teacher education*
21 January 09	Workshop 1: *Reviewing existing scholarship in teacher education research*
25 February 09	Workshop 2: *Theoretical frameworks and their impact on research design: perspectives from psychology, sociology & policy studies*
18 March 09	Workshop 3: *Research methods and designs 1*
20 May 09	Workshop 4: *Qualitative, quantitative and mixed methods*
8 July 09	Workshop 5: *Presentations of group research*

The majority of time at the face-to-face events was given over to the work of the research groups in developing their research designs and devising a research bid to go forward to an appropriate funder. The production of research bids was positioned as a desirable eventual outcome for the research groups' activities, following similar structures implemented in the first year of the WERN. But it has been asserted throughout the TERN project that the main emphasis of the programme is on the quality of the *processes* of professional learning involved, rather than on a final 'product'. Much of the 'value' of the research groups' work is, therefore, conceptualised as offering opportunities for individual and communal learning via the development of an eventual bid. The research mentors play key roles in providing guidance and support to their groups during this process, through their inter-woven roles as mentors, coaches, expert advisers, advocates, mediators and co-learners.

In addition to the allocated planning time at the workshops, groups have dedicated space to collaborate between face-to-face meetings via a series of Virtual Research Environments (VREs). Originally hosted and developed, using the Sakai system, by the TLRP these virtual environments were designed to facilitate communication and exchange of ideas between researchers and to support the systematic development of the research group's bid for funding. The virtual environments also offer the additional benefit of providing storage and easy access to repositories of relevant methodological resources and research literature. Each group has been allocated its own VRE, which it can use as a depository for resources, as a discussion space or chatroom, or to set up wikis for the development of the research proposal. The interactions within the VREs were seen in the original design as supplementing the learning and mentoring which occurred at the face-to-face events. Training was provided at the first three workshops to support effective use of the VREs and technical support was available to cope with the access and technical issues which arose during the project.

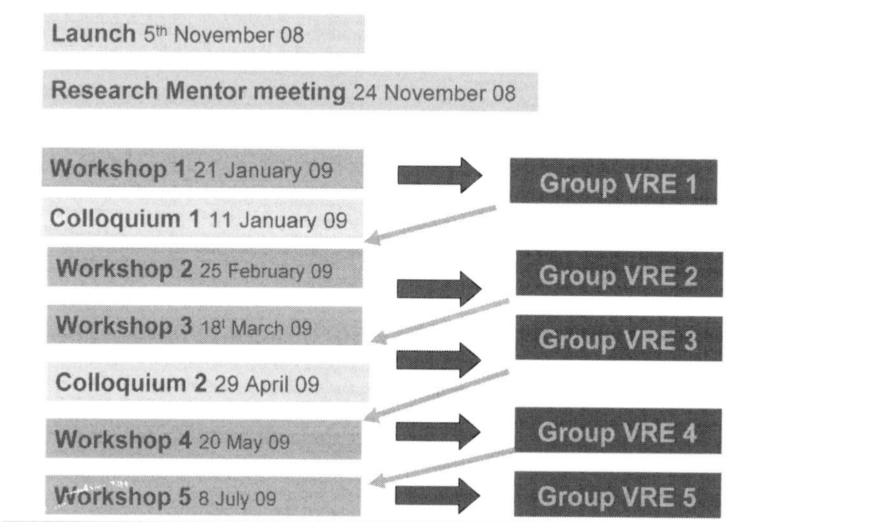

Figure 1. The TERN blended learning programme.

At the start of the programme then, we anticipated that the design of the TERN blended learning programme would enable researchers to create new forms of participation in teacher education research, both through face-to-face and on-line collaborations. Overall, the design and implementation of this blended programme, as a collaborative learning venture between 44 'research aspirant' research fellows and 10 senior researchers as mentors, was meant to draw on individuals' existing knowledge and motivation, with the aim of offering enhanced opportunities for collaborative research and the enhancement of individual and communal expertise. The original ways in which the structure of this learning was envisaged are shown in Figure 1.

Bringing together expertise, motivation and opportunities within TERN: the developing picture

At the time of writing, six events within the programme have occurred. The early data on project engagement show that attendance at face-to-face events has been high, especially in the early stages of the project (86% across the first three events, for example). But degrees of active participation in the project have certainly varied between individuals and across the seven participating universities, as well as across the timeframe of the project. One factor here has been the intensity of work in teacher education, which has meant that institutional imperatives (for example, Ofsted inspections of pre-service courses in some of the universities and management commitments) impacted on some individuals' ability to attend all face-to-face events, as originally planned. Immovable teaching commitments and 'the cloak of busy practicality' in which many teacher educators are said to wrap themselves (Day 1995, 365) may also have been a factor affecting the relatively low rates of participation of four research fellows. Also relevant to consider here is previous research (Larabee 2004; Maguire 2000; Murray 2007), which identifies how teacher educators' values and missions influence the ways in which they conceptualise and balance their research commitments with other aspects of their work.

Individual feedback from fellows and mentors on the content and quality of delivery of the pedagogical inputs at the workshops has been consistently good or very good. At the first workshop, for example, 66% of participants strongly agreed and 34% agreed that the event was a valuable experience which had provided them with an enhanced understanding of existing research in the field of teacher education research in England.

The following data extracts (all taken from internal evaluations of early workshops) indicate some of the ways in which the direct pedagogical inputs within the project have been able to provide opportunities for individual research fellows to develop their understanding of research:

> The role of theory and its connection to data analysis has been highlighted for me through this workshop. It is extremely valuable to listen to experienced researchers and to gain some insights as to their development as researchers.

> I thought that the presentations gave an overview of a range of disciplines which was inspirational. I gained some new knowledge from each of the presenters.

> It made me aware of the large scale pieces of research already conducted in teacher education and the possible gaps.

Other data, also from evaluations of the workshops, illustrate some of the recurring benefits of the opportunities gained through participation in the research groups through both face-to-face meetings and virtual discussions. In addition to growths in professional learning, gathering confidence and on-going motivation are strong themes in these data:

> Following discussion within my own research group, I felt for the first time, I could make a useful contribution to research in this area. The process of selecting a focus for research has been interesting and more complex than I had anticipated.
>
> Liaising with other researchers gives a momentum to my own work and embeds me in a culture of research.
>
> Some of the benefit of being involved in this project is that I realise that I have greater knowledge than I give myself credit for.
>
> It was great to be able to confirm in a constructive, yet critical environment that my ideas were in line with the research aspirations of others. This is particularly beneficial as so often you work in isolation.

Much of the internal data gathered to date give this kind of positive feedback on the project and its associated learning outcomes for individuals. But we would stress that these internal data are still in the very early stages of analysis. We are also aware that there are many methodological, ethical and micro-political issues involved in the gathering and analysis of this kind of internal data, particularly within a regional and institutionally grounded initiative like the TERN project. In addition, we are aware that in a sector, such as teacher education, where opportunities for high quality research development have been limited – in some timeframes and institutional locations at least – by a number of complex factors, the very provision of an ESRC-sponsored, systematic and cross-institutional research development programme is likely to be celebrated by some participants as worthy in its own right.

The evidence beginning to emerge indicates that not all aspects of the programme design have been as successful as the direct inputs. In particular, the VREs have been used more as documentary repositories and less as modes of communication and continuing learning between the face-to-face events. Rather than working in these on-line spaces, some groups have communicated via email, telephone conversations or additional face-to-face meetings rather than via the chat rooms and discussion boards made available in the virtual environments; in other cases annotated word documents emailed backwards and forwards have replaced the on-line wikis as ways of writing the research designs and bids collaboratively.

Across the developing data set, not only have types of individual learning outcomes been varied, but the learning processes and outcomes achieved within each group of researchers are also emerging as differentiated. Initial hypotheses are that these latter differences in particular may be attributable to a number of factors including the size of the group, the types of researcher expertise within it, the chosen focus for the research design/bid and the depth of individual commitment to research this theme over time. The geographical features of the area may also have a part to play in the ways in which the research groups have been able to develop their work. For example, two of the research groups with members based in the universities clustered in and around Liverpool have organised additional face-to-face meetings. These opportunities were not so easy to create for groups which included research fellows from the more geographically isolated University of Cumbria.

In the introduction to this paper we quoted Desforges' equation (cited in Davies and Salisbury 2008, 9) of 'capacity = expertise × motivation × opportunities'. Part of Desforges' argument around this equation was that the use of the multiplier here means that with just one element absent from an initiative the product of the factors of the equation becomes zero (Davies 2008, personal communication). In their paper on the WERN, Davies and Salisbury (2008) draw on external evaluation evidence (Gardner 2008) to argue convincingly that the activities of this network provided all three elements of the equation and were therefore successful in building capacity through this 'multiplier' effect:

> WERN's activities… have given researchers in Wales the *motivation* to engage in research by providing an *opportunity* to develop *expertise* in a supportive and stimulating co-learning environment. (Davies and Salisbury 2008, 9; original emphasis)

With the aforementioned caveats about the nature of the evaluation data and the differentiations within it, the emerging evidence from the TERN project indicates that this initiative too *may* eventually be able to make similar claims in terms of professional learning for at least some of its research fellows. In other words, TERN may have been able to offer differentiated opportunities for research development, enhancement of personal expertise and boosting of motivation to research. Working from Desforges' equation, we *may* therefore be able to claim that individual research capacity was been enhanced in the case of some research fellows on the project. We would also hope that the project has been a learning experience for at least some of the research mentors who, in many ways, have pioneered 'one-to-many' group mentoring techniques within a blended learning programme design.

But to avoid being self-referential, the learning within the project needs to be evaluated in more depth and in ways which are broader and deeper than just a 'within project' focus on individual perceptions and experiences. The research groups, as micro-communal learning structures, and the networked learning that they have involved also require further exploration.

In order to evaluate this learning in more depth we need to consider some potentially difficult issues about the inter-relationships between individual and micro-communal learning within the project. In addition to the hypothetical reasons, posited previously, for the differentiated processes and outcomes, which seem to have been achieved within the research groups, this deeper exploration needs to include considering how the wider project and the specific research groups functioned as networked learning environments (which were – or were not – able to facilitate professional learning to differing degrees), how the mentoring and any models of distributed leadership within the group functioned, and what inter-personal dynamics, academic power relations and levels of trust (or distrust) were influential within the group. These are difficult issues to research, not least because they involve turning the research lens upon ourselves as academics and our practices as researchers, learners, teachers and mentors. But, although methodologically, ethically and (micro)politically challenging to research, the findings of such studies have the potential to illuminate deep and complex issues about teacher educators as an academic (sub)tribe (Becher and Trowler 2002), enabling us to explore patterns of individuality/communality and competition/collaboration in our often tacit practices as researchers in teacher education. Exploring these patterns and the ways in which they relate to the differing discourses and practices of research, scholarship, teaching and service in the very different universities in the project would seem to be an essential part of long-lasting research capacity-building efforts in teacher education.

Significant as gains in professional learning and the development of existing research profiles are for the researchers involved, there are also more ambitious aims for a project like TERN. Capacity building for individuals and micro-communities of researchers is a necessary, but not sufficient in itself, component of broader capacity building at institutional and sector levels. A further level of project evaluation then has to involve identifying how any individual and micro-communal learning within the project has related to the existing teacher education research cultures within the seven universities and to research capacity-building efforts. This is perhaps the hardest level of the evaluation for which to capture and analyse well-grounded data, particularly in the context of such a small-scale project, run over the very limited timeframe of a year. In many ways it is far too soon to see any discernable impact of the project on the varied institutional cultures within the seven universities. But in order to begin to explore this level of the project's 'reach' (that is, how widely the project has or has not been disseminated internally) into the education faculties of the seven universities, interviews at the end of the funded project are planned with research leaders in each university. These interviews will aim to gather data about institutional participation in and commitment to the project and to analyse its 'reach' at institutional level. This aspect of the project will be the focus of further analysis and writing, once the first year of the project is completed.

Conclusions

As stated in the introduction to this article, TERN was originally funded for only one academic year, a very short funding period for such an ambitious project. That funding is now nearing its end. But since the project's inception in summer 2008, discussions have taken place across the seven universities about longer-term sustainability. By late spring 2009 it was clear that there was considerable regional and national interest in sustaining some version of the project beyond the formal end of the ESRC funding. This interest was in part attributable to developing evidence of first, the impact on the region, in the form of subsidiary networks and research groupings developing from the original project and second, increased levels of participation in other regional events. The deans of the seven universities, the Steering Group and the majority of the participants have now resolved that the project should be continued into a second year. Participant feedback on sustainability has indicated that 92% of the research fellows and mentors surveyed to date would like to be involved in a second year of the project (with 8% supporting the idea of sustainability but 'not sure' of their individual commitment). The majority of participants would like to maintain the pattern of regular face-to-face events and group projects. The group also recommended that the network be opened to new participants from the seven regional universities in its second year. We are therefore now planning for a second year of activity, which will sustain the network into 2010, and hopefully beyond.

The challenges for research capacity building in teacher education research in England were discussed at the beginning of this article. It is clearly unrealistic to see the immediate outcomes of a small-scale project like TERN, involving only 54 participants, having a direct impact on strengthening research capacity across teacher education, which in many ways is such a beleaguered sector of higher education in

England. But, as indicated at the beginning of this article, one of the main aims of the project was to test the potential of this model for building an infrastructure to strengthen teacher education research on a larger scale across England. At the time of writing there is interest in developing other regional networks, on broadly similar models to the TERN project; in London and two other regions of England. There is also interest in implementing such initiatives in Scotland and Northern Ireland. It is very early days yet for the transformation of initial interest into well-articulated and operational networks in other regions/nations, but the potential replication of the TERN model may be one way in which the project can contribute to research capacity building within the teacher education sector.

In terms of the TERN project itself our hope is still that the model will enable at least some of its participating researchers to ground their personal research expertise and motivations in collaborative endeavours, thus contributing to the strengthening of individual and collaborative capacity in the North West region. We certainly envisage that TERN will play some role in accelerating the career development of a new wave of teacher education researchers in the North West institutions. But in the long-term the success of the project in the North West, and in any other regions where a similar model may be developed in future, will clearly be dependent on the ways in which it is able to build, collaboratively and strategically, on the particular strengths of the individual teacher educators who participate in it, on the learning they achieve in the micro-communities of their research groups and, crucially perhaps, on the congruence which this learning has with the existing cultures of research, scholarship and teaching in the departments of education within which they work. Of central importance here, we suggest, is how the relationships between research, scholarship and teaching are understood and enacted individually and institutionally (Deem and Lucas 2007; Larabee 2004; Nixon 1996; Sikes 2006).

The TERN project, as this article has indicated, has been designed to contribute specifically to the research capacity-building agenda in terms of strengthening individual researcher expertise, building micro-communal and regional research networks and developing institutional research capacity in teacher education. We would acknowledge, however, that of equal importance is the development of high-quality work in this area of education research. As indicated in the introduction, there is a clear need in the UK and beyond to address issues around the current types of research predominant in and on teacher education (Cochran-Smith and Zeichner 2006; Menter et al. forthcoming; Richardson 2007), not least to enable us to maintain and develop research-informed models of pre- and in-service teacher education.

Analyses relating to the issue of quality in the TERN project will follow in due course when more extensive evaluation and review has been undertaken. We began this article by acknowledging that the TERN project is very much work in progress. We finish our paper on a similar note by emphasising that the issues raised here are in need of further and much more in-depth exploration, both by the project team and within the general work on research capacity building in education currently being undertaken by BERA and the Strategic Forum for Research in Education.

Note

1. There are three broad types of university referred to in this article: (1) pre-1992 or 'old' universities (also known as 'established' or 'charter' universities, which were granted

university status by charter at some point before 1992; (2) the post-1992 or 'new' universities (also known as 'statute' universities) were in the main previously polytechnics, granted university status in 1992; (3) post-2000 universities (previously colleges of higher education, as diversified HE providers, granted university by statute sometime after 2000). This third group therefore includes the UK's newest universities. As indicated in the article, four of the universities in the TERN project come into this third category.

References

Baron, S. 2005. TLRP's phase 2 research capacities building strategy. *Research Intelligence* 93: 14–17.

Becher, T., and P. Trowler. 2002. *Academic tribes and territories: Intellectual enquiry and the culture of disciplines.* Buckingham, UK: SRHE and OUP.

Boyd, P., L. Baker, K. Harris, C. Kynch, and E. McVittie. 2005. Working with multiple identities: Supporting new teacher education tutors in higher education. Paper presented at the British Educational Research Association Conference, September, at the University of Glamorgan, Pontypridd.

British Educational Research Association. 2006. Presentation at Special Interest Group Convenors Meeting at the BERA Annual Conference, 6–9 September, in Warwick.

British Educational Research Association. 2008. Presentation at Special Interest Group Convenors Meeting at the BERA Annual Conference, 3–6 September, at Heriot Watt University, Edinburgh.

Cochran-Smith, M., and K. Zeichner, eds. 2006. *Studying teacher education: The report of the AERA panel on research and teacher education.* Washington, DC: AERA and Lawrence Erlbaum Associates.

Cochran-Smith, M., and K. Demers. 2008. How do we know what we know? Research and teacher education. In *Handbook of research on teacher education,* ed. M. Cochran-Smith, S. Feiman-Nemser, D.J. McIntyre and K. Demers, 1009–16. New York: Routledge/Taylor Francis and the Association of Teacher Educators.

Dadds, M., and C. Kynch. 2003. The impact of the RAE 3b rating on educational research in teacher education departments. *Research Intelligence* 84: 8–11.

Davies, S., and J. Salisbury. 2008. Researching and learning together: Inter-institutional collaboration as a strategy for capacity building. Paper presented at the British Educational Research Conference (BERA), 3–6 September, at Heriot Watt University, Edinburgh.

Day, C. 1995. Qualitative research, professional development and the role of teacher educators: Fitness for purpose. *British Educational Research Journal* 21, no. 3: 135–49.

Deem, R., and L. Lucas. 2007. Research and teaching work within university education departments: Fragmentation or integration. *Journal of Further and Higher Education* 31, no. 1: 17–29.

Dyson, A., and C. Desforges. 2002. Building research capacity: Some possible lines of action. National Educational Research Forum Working Paper 1.1

Economic and Social Research Council. 2006. *Demographic review of the social sciences.* Swindon, UK: ESRC.

Erixon Arreman, I. 2008. The process of finding a shape: Stabilizing new research structures in Swedish Teacher Education (2000–2007). *European Educational Research Journal* 7, no. 2: 321–33.

Fowler, Z., and R. Procter. 2008. Mapping the ripples: An evaluation of TLRP's research capacity building. http://www.tlrp.org/mappingtheripples (accessed August 7, 2008).

Furlong, J. 2005. New Labour and teacher education. *Oxford Review of Education* 31, no. 2: 119–34.

Furlong, J. 2007. The universities and education: Where are we? How did we get here? Where should we be? Keynote address to the University Council for the Education of Teachers Annual Conference, 9–10 November, in Staverton, UK.

Furlong, J. 2009. Life after the Research Assessment Exercise: Research and teacher education. Presentation to the University Council for the Education of Teachers, Research and Development Committee, April 30.

Furlong, J., L. Barton, S. Miles, C. Whiting, and G. Whitty. 2000. *Teacher education in transition.* Buckingham, UK: OUP.

Gardner, J. 2008. *The Welsh Educational Research Network: An evaluation.* Belfast, NI: Queens' University School of Education.

Gilroy, P., and O. McNamara. 2009. A critical history of research assessment in the United Kingdom and its post-1992 impact on education. *Journal of Education for Teaching* 35, no. 4: 321–35.

Harrison, J., and F. McKeon. 2008. The early research career development of beginning teacher educators – a case study approach. Paper presented at the European Educational Research Conference, 10–12 September, in Gothenburg, Sweden.

HERO. 2008. Education panel report RAE 2008. http://www.hero.ac.uk/sites/hero/rae/overview/docs/UoA45.doc (accessed March 24, 2009).

Larabee, D. 2004. *The trouble with ed schools.* New York: Yale University Press.

Lawn, M., and J. Furlong. 2007. The social organisation of educational research in England. *European Educational Research Journal* 6, no. 1: 55–70.

Maguire, M. 2000. Inside/outside the ivory tower: Teacher education in the English academy. *Teaching in Higher Education* 5, no. 2: 149–65.

McIntyre, D. and A. McIntyre. 1999. Capacity for research into teaching and learning. http://www.tlrp.org/dspace/handle/123456789/330 (accessed January 12, 2006).

McNamara, O., M. Brundrett, and R. Webb. 2008. *Primary Review Interim Reports, Research Survey 6/3. Primary teachers: Initial teacher education, continuing professional development and school leadership development.* Cambridge, UK: University of Cambridge.

Menter, I., E. Brisard, and I. Smith. 2006. *Convergence or divergence? Initial teacher education in Scotland and England.* Edinburgh, UK: Dunedin Academic Press.

Menter, I., M. Hulme, M. Jones, J. Murray, A. Campbell, I. Hextall, P. Mahony, R. Procter, and K. Wall. Forthcoming. Teacher education research in the UK: The state of the art. *Swiss Revue of Educational Research.*

Munn, P. 2008. BERA Presidential Address: Building research capacity collaboratively: Can we take ownership of our future? *British Educational Research Journal* 34, no. 4: 413–30.

Murray, J. 2007. Countering insularity in teacher education. Academic work on pre-service courses in nursing, social work and teacher education. *Journal of Education for Teaching* 33, no. 3: 271–91.

Murray, J. 2008. Teacher educators' induction into higher education: Work-based learning in the micro communities of teacher education. *European Journal of Teacher Education* 31, no. 2: 117–33.

Murray, J., A. Campbell, I. Hextall, M. Hulme, M. Jones, P. Mahony, I. Menter, R. Procter, and K. Wall. 2008. Mapping the field of teacher education research: Methodology and issues in a research-capacity building initiative in teacher education in the UK. *European Educational Research Journal* 7, no. 4: 459–74.

Murray, J., A. Campbell, I. Hextall, M. Hulme, M. Jones, P. Mahony, I. Menter, R. Procter, and K. Wall. 2009. Research and teacher education in the UK: Building capacity. *Teachers and Teacher Education* 25: 944–50.

Murray, J., and P. Mahony. 2009. On learning from the research successful. Cass School of Education, University of East London and School of Education, Roehampton University. (in preparation).

Nixon, J. 1996. Professional identity and the restructuring of higher education. *Studies in Higher Education* 21, no. 2: 5–16.

Pollard, A. 2007. Editorial: The UK's teaching and learning research programme: Findings and significance. *British Educational Research Journal* 33, no. 5: 639–46.

Pollard, A. 2008. Towards new strategic initiatives for research capacity in education: A discussion paper. *Building Research Capacity* 13: 1–5.

Rees, G., S. Baron, R. Boyask, and C. Taylor. 2007. Research-capacity building professional learning and the social practices of educational research. *British Educational Research Journal* 33, no. 5: 761–79.

Richardson, V. 2007. Research on teacher education: Past, present and future. Paper presented at the University of Michigan 2006–2007 Seminar Series on Teacher Education, March, in Ann Arbour, MI.

Shulman, L. 1999. Professing educational scholarship. In *Issues in education research: Problems and possibilities,* ed. E. Lagemann and L. Shulman, 159–65. San Francisco, CA: Jossey Bass.

Sikes, P. 2006. Working in a 'new' university: In the shadow of the Research Assessment Exercise. *Studies in Higher Education* 31, no. 5: 234–52.

Building capacity through teacher enquiry: the Scottish Schools of Ambition

Moira Hulme[a], Vivienne Baumfield[a] and Fran Payne[b]

[a]*Faculty of Education, University of Glasgow, Glasgow, UK;* [b]*School of Education, University of Aberdeen, Aberdeen, UK*

There has been much recent interest in collaboration and networking within and between schools to promote innovation, school improvement, and professional development. This paper starts with a brief review of the recent history of teacher research in the UK in order to consider how pre- and in-service teachers are currently positioned in relation to research. Drawing on the case of the Scottish *Schools of Ambition*, a network of 52 schools receiving additional resource for targeted school improvement, the paper identifies some of the challenges and opportunities presented by sponsored research engagement. Tensions between evaluating and being supportive when engaged in an externally sponsored initiative with the specific goal of demonstrating school improvement are highlighted. The perception that any change in modes of working tends to be more visible in the institutional context of school rather than the university is also noted. Based on the experience of this Scottish case and a review of current research into school–university partnerships, we argue that effective collaborations need to address questions of power to ensure mutual benefits, reciprocity, and a genuine coalition of interest amongst partners. The paper suggests that teacher educators may have an important contribution to make to building capacity through teacher enquiry given their position as mediators between schools and university faculties of education.

Introduction

Within the literature, several terms with different meanings are used, often interchangeably, to describe teacher enquiry. Lassonde and Israel (2008, 7) identify common ground in their assertion that, 'Teacher research is a type of *action research*, is synonymous with *teacher inquiry*, shares many characteristics with *practitioner inquiry*, and incorporates *reflective teaching* and *critical reflective practice*'. For the purposes of this paper, we refer to teacher research defined by Cochran-Smith and Lytle (1993, 7) as 'systematic and intentional inquiry carried out by teachers'.

The teacher research movement has a distinguished history in the UK. Craig (2009, 62) has argued that 'the British curriculum reform movement birthed the concept of teacher as researcher'. Interest in teachers as researchers was promoted through the work of Stenhouse in the late 1960s, and Elliot and Adelman in the 1970s. The Australian action research movement, with a stronger critical perspective, developed under the influence of Kemmis in the late 1970s and 1980s. In North America, Schwab, like Stenhouse, sought to enhance teachers' participation in curriculum deliberation, whilst Schön (1983) advanced the now established 'reflective turn' in teacher preparation and development. In Central and South America, 'Freirean-inspired participatory research' emerged to challenge existing hierarchies of knowledge production (Anderson, Herr and Nihlen 1994, 17). Teacher research is thus an international movement at different stages of development and informed by different ideologies. Across these diverse strands, there is a common commitment to inquiry done by teachers (and other practitioners) to inform improvement action.

The recent history of teacher research is influenced by enhanced attention internationally to teacher collaboration and the potential of teacher research networks to support professional development, school improvement and systemic change within school systems (Craig 2009; Rönnerman, Furu and Salo 2008). The political legitimation of teacher research as a re-professionalising strategy has raised concern among some of its strongest proponents who question whether the discourse of teacher research is being appropriated to enhance self-regulation of the school workforce and intensify teachers' work (Elliot 2001; Altrichter and Gstettner 1993).

In the UK, much debate in the last decade has centred on the need to strengthen the relationship between teachers, educational researchers, and policy makers. The active promotion of teacher research within policy circles in the late 1990s was accompanied by claims that funded educational research conducted within universities ought to satisfy the key criteria of 'usability' and 'credibility'. The relevance and quality of educational research was subject to criticism in high-profile reports (Tooley and Darby 1998; Hillage et al. 1998). Subsequently, commissioned educational research was aligned closely with central policy agenda and more attentive to the professional user perspective.

The promotion of teacher research is thus enmeshed in debates about professional knowledge and different interpretations of what constitute appropriate 'evidence' and legitimate 'knowledge' and 'knowers'. An official commitment to enhance teachers' professionalism by formally encouraging teachers' engagement in and with research in the UK was at the same time a critique of the professional research community, a debate further contextualised by the renegotiation of relations between university personnel (as 'providers of services') and schools (as 'clients') (Day 2007). Moreover, educational research is a 'broad church' encompassing basic, applied, and developmental research (Strategic Forum for Research in Education 2008). The level of engagement by practitioners with the diverse forms of educational research proceeds against a backdrop wherein teacher preparation has become more strongly oriented towards technical teaching skills whilst couched in a discourse of 'professionalisation' (Menter 2009).

Teacher educators are uniquely positioned in the school–university, research–practice nexus. Whilst drawing on extensive professional expertise, research training and sustained engagement in research may be less secure among university teachers appointed to teacher education posts. This may be especially pertinent in the 'new' university sector (post-1992), which has been less likely to attract core research funding (Sikes 2006). It is widely recognised that capacity building for teacher education within university departments of education is a national and international priority (Murray et al. 2009; Munn 2008; Cochran-Smith and Zeichner 2006). It is one of the tensions within the discourse on evidence-informed practice that research funding has become increasingly 'selective' and concentrated, as research engagement is encouraged to be distributed and expansive (Furlong 2004). We argue here that promotion of research-informed teaching depends on the relations of partnership fostered between university departments of education and schools (and indeed between teacher educators and educational researchers); and that much rests on the provision of opportunities for professional development that support professional enquiry, research and scholarship across university and school communities. In forging these relationships, sensitivity to the micro-political dimensions of partnerships and how these are framed by the wider policy context are significant.

Professional enquiry and teacher education

Practitioner research is one form of professional enquiry. Much attention in all four jurisdictions of the UK is focused on promoting career-long professional learning to provide coherence across five professional 'milestones' of teachers' careers. Thus Northern Ireland's Professional Development Framework has five developmental 'milestones': Initial Teacher Education; Induction; Early Professional Development; Chartered Teacher; and Advanced Chartered Teacher (General Teaching Council for Northern Ireland [GTCNI] 2005). Wales' General Teaching Council (GTC) has also recommended a Professional Development Framework with five milestones: Qualified Teacher Status (QTS); Induction; Middle Leader; Chartered Teacher; and Senior Leader/Headship (General Teaching Council for Wales 2006). In England, the framework for professional standards for teachers similarly identifies five career stages: award of QTS; Induction; Post-threshold Teachers; Excellent Teachers; and Advanced Skills Teachers (Training and Development Agency [TDA] 2007). In Scotland, the GTC for Scotland is considering strengthening the four existing standards: Provisional Registration; Induction/Full Registration; Chartered Teacher; and the Standard for Headship; with additional leadership standards to 'complete a suite of teaching standards which will provide guidance for teachers across their careers' (Tony Finn, Chief Executive General Teaching Council for Scotland [GTCS], quoted on page 4 of *Teaching Scotland* on January 28, 2009).

It is therefore no surprise that there is some divergence in orientation towards enquiry within the professional standards across the UK, which reflects different arrangements for the governance and regulation of teacher education (Hulme and Menter 2008). In England, an incremental approach is taken to research engagement as the basis for evidence-informed change. Beginning teachers are required to adopt 'a creative and constructively critical approach towards innovation' (TDA 2007, 8), whereas experienced and accomplished teachers, who meet the criteria for the Excellent Teacher grade introduced in 2006, are required to, 'Research and evaluate innovative curricular practices and draw on research outcomes and other sources of external evidence to inform their own practice and that of colleagues' (TDA 2007, 27). Although the Northern Ireland teaching competences do not make explicit reference to research, engagement in and with research is integral to the GTCNI's (2007) philosophy of teaching as a 'reflective and activist profession'. 'Teachers should engage in action research within their own classroom, school or institution and, in addition, they should take cognisance of research within the broader education community' (GTCNI 2007, 11).

Research engagement is embedded within the professional development framework for teachers in Scotland (Kirkwood and Christie 2006). Teacher education in Scotland is university-led and the GTCS has ownership of the professional standards. There is an expectation that, from an early stage in professional formation, Scottish teachers will use 'research and other forms of valid evidence to inform choice, change and priorities in promoting educational practices and progress' (GTCS 2006, 4). On successful completion of the induction year via the Teacher Induction Scheme (this was introduced in Scotland in August 2002 and offers a guaranteed one-year salaried training post with a maximum class commitment of 0.7 full-time equivalent and dedicated time for professional development), the *Standard for Full Registration* requires new teachers to have 'research-based knowledge relating to learning and teaching and a critical appreciation of the contribution of research to education in general' (GTCS 2006, 11). Recent research has indicated that early career teachers in Scotland (in the first five years of their teaching careers) demonstrate positive attitudes to professional development through research engagement (Hulme et al. 2008).

A commitment to 'critical self-evaluation and development' is one of the core professional values and personal commitments within the *Standard for Chartered Teachers* (GTCS 2002, 1). The Chartered Teacher Programme was introduced in August 2003 and is open to all teachers who have reached the top of the main grade teachers' pay scale and who have maintained a continuing professional development (CPD) portfolio. Progression through the Chartered Teacher grade is by qualification i.e. progression through a self-funded 12-module Master's degree. The Scottish Chartered Teacher is required to demonstrate a capacity to 'evaluate practice and reflect critically on it' and to 'ensure that teaching is based on reading and research' (GTCS 2002, 10). Similarly, the pilot Welsh Chartered Teacher programme, to be funded by the Welsh Assembly Government and piloted between 2007 and 2009, aims to combine standards relevant to classroom practice and middle leadership to position the Chartered Teacher as a leader of learning (although it should be noted that unlike the Scottish and the English schemes, the Welsh Chartered Teacher status is not a pay-related standard).

A review of standards documents across the UK suggests a developing expectation that 'accomplished' teachers will draw on research and other sources of evidence to inform and improve their own practice and that of others. Whilst espoused commitments to research engagement are found within the professional standards for teachers, opportunities, and support for pedagogic enquiry remain patchy. For experienced teachers engaging in award bearing courses the challenge of becoming a teacher-researcher can be considerable. There is consensus among directors of the Chartered Teacher Programme across university providers in Scotland that experienced teachers often struggle to adopt a research orientation when reflecting on their own practice. This suggests a need for sustained and deepening engagement across the career phases.

Sponsored teacher research in the UK

Opportunities for serving teachers to undertake research-based enquiry over the last decade (beyond award bearing courses) have tended to be through the award of small grants to 'lone scholars' (Furlong, Salisbury and Coombs 2003). An espoused commitment to the development of new partnerships between higher education and 'teachers-as-researchers' was officially promoted in England and Wales through the Teacher Research Grant Scheme (1997–2001) followed by the Best Practice Research Scholarship Programme (2000–2004). Both schemes gave small grants to teachers to undertake 'classroom focused small-scale studies in priority areas' (Department for Education and Employment 2000, 1). Practitioner enquiry continues to be endorsed through the General Teaching Council for England's Teacher Learning Academy and the National College of School Leadership's Research Associates Programme.

Outside England and Wales, the Scottish Council for Research in Education (SCRE) has a long tradition of supporting teacher research. Founded in 1928 by the Educational Institute of Scotland (the teachers' union) in partnership with local education authorities, SCRE was influential in shaping the early relationship between teachers and research and strengthening connections between research and policy in Scotland (Lawn 2004). Now the 'SCRE Centre' within the Faculty of Education of the University of Glasgow, SCRE no longer receives central funds for these activities but support for teacher researchers in Scotland continues on a small-scale in a variety of forms. The Scottish Teachers for a New Era (STNE) programme (see Gray et al. in this issue) based at Aberdeen University operates a Teacher Action Research Scholarship Scheme. The GTCS offers small grants through a modest Teacher Researcher Programme and encourages professional recognition for enquiry-based contributions to school development.

Support for teacher research in Northern Ireland and Wales is similarly piecemeal and varied. Leitch (2008, 110) suggests, 'Practitioner research in Northern Ireland is significantly underdeveloped, under-recognised and until recently uncoordinated'. In addition to university-based teacher education programmes, there is some provision for school-based action research supported by the GTCNI, the Curriculum Advisory and Support Services, and the Learning and Skills Development Agency. From 2001, under the provisions of the national programme for CPD, teachers in Wales are eligible to apply for small grants to conduct action research projects with support from an appropriate mentor within a higher education institution, subject association, or local authority.

Across the UK opportunities for sponsored elective forms of practitioner enquiry have tended to be time-bound programmes to support lone researchers in single cycle enquiries. Evaluations of teacher research programmes have identified the limitations of such an approach. Principal among these are weaknesses in research design and methodology, a tendency to over-claim (Foster 1999), absence of systematic reviews of literature (Furlong, Salisbury and Coombs 2003), weak report writing and dissemination strategies (James and Egan 2004) and lack of clarity surrounding criteria for judging quality (Furlong and Oancea 2006). Entry to these schemes affords individual teachers access to a 'discourse' of research, with the support of an external mentor, that might 'augment their practice' (Furlong 2004), but may not promote a level of research engagement likely to satisfy aspirations for teaching (collectively) as a research and evidence-informed profession. Supporters of teacher research point to the need for more sustained engagement than is possible within the confines of three school terms and the need for research priorities that encourage teachers to engage critically with the 'act of teaching' *and* the 'context of teaching' (Prestage, Perks and Soares 2003, 62).

School–university collaboration to support teacher enquiry

We have acknowledged a growing emphasis on teachers' use and production of research and the revision of professional standards to promote development, reflection and enquiry as professional attributes across the career phases. We have also noted a long history of research by teachers that has been largely small-scale and fragmented in development, despite rhetorical claims that such work is intended to influence decisions about effective practice at policy levels. Renewed interest in practitioner research and the embedding of enquiry within professional standards (to a greater or lesser extent across the UK), has proceeded alongside enhanced attention to organisational learning as a basis for systemic improvement. It is to the theme of collaboration that we now turn.

Based on a review of literature published over a 20-year period in the USA, Canada and Australia, Ravid and Handler (2001) have identified four models of school–university collaboration:

(1) the *professional development* school model for pre-service teacher education;
(2) the *consultation* model to support school improvement and teacher professional development;
(3) the *one-to-one collaboration* model involving school and university collaborators as co-researchers; and
(4) the *umbrella* model involving multiple team collaboration through a central facilitating organisation.

Support for sponsored teacher research in the UK is largely consistent with the consultation model, based on contractual relations. Most *school* research networks (as opposed to networks supporting individual practitioner researchers) are funded directly through government channels and are managed through steering groups. One example of such an approach would be the Scottish Educational Research Association's (SERA) Emerging Researchers Network which aims to support beginning practitioner researchers in Scottish universities, schools and colleges. Examples of sponsored research collaborations in the United Kingdom include the School-Based Research Consortia initiative (1998–2001), the Research Engaged Schools Programme (2003–2005) and the Networked Learning Communities Programme (2000–2006). In addition, long-standing local research partnerships founded on consultation have grown from initial teacher education partnerships, notably the Schools–University Partnership for Educational Research supported by the University of Cambridge, Faculty of Education (McLaughlin et al. 2006).

Until recently, much of the work on school–university partnerships has been under-theorised, especially in terms of the power relations between participants. In contrast, studies in other areas of public policy have problematised the 'will to empower' (Cruikshank 1999) and noted a sometimes fine distinction between ownership, colonisation, collusion and co-option. Critical policy studies have sought to position discourses of collaboration alongside wider accountability and efficiency concerns (Ozga and Walker 1995). These studies remind us that the attractions of 'participatory reforms' do not negate serious consideration of power relations and status inequities (Anderson 1999). An understanding of 'practice' as relational, and thus 'collaboration' as social practice and 'networking' as activity, enables connections to be made with established work that has highlighted the varying *degrees* of collaboration (Hargreaves 1994) and the micro-political tensions inherent in school culture and organisation (Ball 1987).

The Schools of Ambition programme – a Scottish case

The Schools of Ambition programme (2006–2010) is distinctive in Scotland in its promotion of a teacher enquiry model within a national programme for school change. The policy document *Ambitious, excellent schools* (Scottish Executive Education Department [SEED] 2004) set out the modernisation agenda for Scotland's comprehensive schools. Within a framework of national guidance, schools were encouraged to explore flexible, creative and innovative approaches to school improvement (Learning and Teaching Scotland 2003). The Schools of Ambition programme was at the forefront of these developments, designed 'to bring about a step change in ambition and achievement' (SEED 2004, 12). Fifty-two (mainly secondary) schools have embarked on a three-year programme of planned change since the launch of the programme. Many of the schools are engaged in curriculum restructuring as a result of new flexibility afforded in recent policy. Each school is receiving additional funding (£100,000 per annum) to implement a locally negotiated 'transformational plan'. The 52 schools are distributed across Scotland's 32 local authorities, and include those at the forefront of leading innovation and change, and others considered to be in need of 'transformation' following school inspections.

Following a process of competitive tendering, a consortium of the Universities of Glasgow, Aberdeen and Strathclyde was awarded the contract for Research to Support Schools of Ambition.[1] There are two strands to this work. The first involves streaming formative feedback to the schools and the provision of mentor support for practitioner research undertaken through the Schools of Ambition programme. One mentor supports each school and the majority of mentors support more than one school. The second strand involves examining the processes of change across the network of schools. The university team has sought to promote reflexivity as an integral aspect of participation in this project. To this end, an experienced researcher within the lead university, but outside the project team, has supported the development of a supplementary 'reflexive strand' to this work.

In addition to the university-based mentors, a team of advisers seconded from local authority advisory services supports the schools. The advisers provide linkage and improve the flow of communication between the schools and other strands of the policy community such as Learning and Teaching Scotland (the main organisation for the development of the Scottish school curriculum), the schools' Inspectorate and local authority officers. Whereas the mentors and advisers share a common commitment to building capacity, they have different roles and responsibilities within the programme. Mentors focus on the development of systematic professional enquiry and advisers monitor and support school compliance with programme objectives.

The mentoring role encompasses a range of activities including advice on:

- issues of manageability/scope of work, stages, timeline and resources;
- ethical practice in practitioner research;
- collaborative use of a bespoke Virtual Research Environment;
- accessing electronic resources and Web links to support practitioner enquiry
- support for refining teacher-initiated proposals;

- data collection and analysis;
- monitoring and self-evaluation;
- dissemination of work in progress, writing enquiry summaries and in compiling the school's final report, the 'Telling the Story' portfolio (University of Glasgow 2008).

In order to meet the diverse needs of each school, a programme of support tailored to individual needs is negotiated. Support is provided via face-to-face meetings during scheduled school visits and online via the Virtual Research Environment. In addition, the Scottish government national team of advisers convenes regional networking events and the Research Support Team organises an annual Schools of Ambition evaluation conference. This event provides a supportive environment for teachers to share activities and access a range of training workshops designed to support practitioner research. The 2009 conference invited participation from local authorities and school personnel outside the School of Ambition community.

In contrast to small grant schemes for individual teachers, whole-school and cross-school projects have stressed the significance of 'School Enquiry Groups' or 'School Improvement Groups' (McLaughlin et al. 2006; Street and Temperley 2005). Within the framework for Schools of Ambition, the term 'evaluation group' was adopted. Not all schools were receptive to the idea of forming an evaluation group and progress across the network has been varied. The need for project management was met through delegation to senior colleagues in schools, most commonly deputy headteachers (assistant principals) (who already carry multiple responsibilities) or through the creation of (temporary) project manager or evaluation coordinator posts from among the school staff. In a minority of cases, the headteacher assumed responsibility for conducting evaluation activities as part of their strategic leadership of the programme of transformation. Where this was the case, accounts reveal that this was motivated by workload concerns in schools with limited capacity to create additional resource to support evaluation responsibilities. It is perhaps worth noting that these developments were taking place in the context of the continuing implementation of *A Teaching Profession for the 21st Century*, the McCrone Agreement, where studies have shown teachers to be continuing to experience considerable workloads (Audit Scotland 2006; Menter et al. 2006; HM Inspectorate of Education [HMIe] 2007).

Building and sustaining relations of partnership across the three groups of participants (and negotiating commitments to each) has been an unsteady process. By the end of the second year (June 2008), 15 of the 28 schools (54%) participating in the programme at that time had formed an evaluation group with up to eight members (University of Glasgow 2008). This process was sometimes interrupted by recurrent changes in school staff; varying degrees of preparedness to devolve opportunities beyond school management teams; negative connotations attached to 'research' and its relevance to the pragmatic concerns of class teachers, and suspicion about the role of 'evaluation' within school, especially in relation to peer observation. School leaders commonly acted as gatekeepers, moderating the transfer of new practices from 'outside' collaborators and thus constraining the process.

Teachers in non-promoted posts were keen to avoid disruption to their classes (especially certificate classes) or additional 'cover' requirements for peers to enable them to attend support meetings and undertake evaluation activities. To resolve the dilemma of time use, meetings were often held in 'free' periods, working lunches or twilight sessions after school, with the risk of further exacerbating a perception of systematic enquiry as a significant additional 'bolt on' commitment. Incentives for engagement were commonly offered through internal bids for additional departmental funds and, in one case, through personal honoraria in recognition of the additional work undertaken by teacher researchers recruited to a school evaluation group. Where ethical issues have arisen, these have tended to relate to the degree of self-determination of research activities achievable within existing school decision-making structures. This was particularly pointed where delegation of tasks was justified by the appeal of 'distributed leadership'.

The limitations of externally imposed or 'contrived collegiality' (Hargreaves 1994) are well documented. Mentor engagement requires sensitivity to the many competing demands on busy teachers' time, and a preparedness to work flexibly within the shifting timescales that mark the peak and troughs of evaluation activity across the school calendar. Throughout this process, it was important to maintain 'critical' friendship in providing feedback to scaffold further reflection, development and improvement action. Grundy, Robison and Tomazos (2001, 209) have described the mentor's task as involving the careful exercise of professional judgment, constantly toggling between 'interventionist' and 'facilitative' roles. Perry, Komesaroff and Kavanagh (2002) have emphasised the importance of valuing small-scale incremental change in an effort to maintain momentum during inevitable times of turbulence and periodic stasis. The Schools of Ambition initiative coincided with major reform of the school curriculum and a review of the National Qualifications Framework in Scotland. A research approach to evaluation was thus prescient but was also perceived to intensify demands on lead practitioners in some schools. Our experience in supporting teachers has varied across the schools. When schools have been less responsive, maintaining a balance between the interventionist and facilitative aspects of the 'critical friend' role has not been easy.

Extending the activity of the evaluation groups beyond routine quantitative data gathering (attendance, attainment, exclusion and participation rates) to include consideration of 'soft' (qualitative) indicators and the involvement of students (and other stakeholders) as co-investigators has proven particularly challenging for university mentors. Encouraging school partners acculturated to a 'discourse of delivery' (Fielding 2003), many of whom have little previous experience of educational research and evaluation, to postpone judgement in the knowledge that there are 'no quick fixes' (Stoll and Meyers 1998) has proven similarly challenging. The diverse nature of the schools with their very different starting points and reasons for becoming a School of Ambition is an additional factor. As the partnership has developed, we have encouraged the promotion of an action research model. In doing so, a distinction has been made between doing a time-bound work-based project and adopting an 'inquiry stance' to professional practice (Cochran-Smith and Lytle 2009).

The involvement of several of the schools in concurrent rounds of targeted School of Ambition inspections or repeat inspections by HMIe, the Scottish schools inspectorate, has further complicated challenging local circumstances. The policy rhetoric around Schools of Ambition, which encourages innovation and managed risk taking, proceeds alongside powerful forms of accountability that continue to draw on conventional performance indicators. Despite the promotion of devolved forms of school self-evaluation by the schools' inspectorate from 1996 (for guidance documents and toolkits see HMIe [2006]), school leaders felt that a hierarchy of evidence (from 'hard' to 'soft', external to internal generation) would be used in appraising their progress and this influenced the choice of enquiry strategy that school personnel were encouraged to develop.

University researchers working collaboratively with practitioner researchers in schools in partnerships have been characterised as participating in a form of 'precarious organization' in which marginality is both a source of strength and tension (Miller 2001). Maintaining relationships in such unstable contexts demands a high level of flexibility and this requires a commitment to spending time on fostering and sustaining the personal relationships that enable the partnership to prosper:

> Negotiation was… essential and depended crucially on mutual understanding of different needs and purposes, and willingness to give and take criticism as part of the development process. Possibly this kind of open relationship, which is inevitably personal as well as professional, can only be achieved over a considerable period of time. (James and Worrall 2000, 95)

Day and Hadfield (2004) highlight the importance of trust as a vital element for partnership working to be successful, both between teachers working in action research networks across schools, and between organisations who support capacity building and learning networks.

Tripp (1998, 41) identified four types of (power) relationships that are typically forged in school–university partnerships: *consenting*, where the teacher is positioned as 'researched subject'; *consulting*, where the teacher is positioned as actor/informer; *cooperative*, where the teacher is informer/reflector; and *collaborative*, which is characterised by shared control of a research process where both parties are co-researchers. In switching between the dual roles of external research team (to map the on-going process of change across the schools) and supporters of school enquiry (within a small cluster of schools), the Schools of Ambition mentors have engaged with teachers across the full spectrum of positions identified by Tripp (1998), shifting between roles and positions in line with the research brief at different points in the project calendar, though always aspiring to the maintenance of cooperative relations.

Conclusion

The interest of policy-makers in partnerships, collaborations and networks in the public sector is often presented in terms of fostering innovation and the formation of new relationships and systems of working. However, tensions can arise where questions of who has power, who gains and who loses are left unanswered or even unasked (Lowndes and Skelcher 1998). A commitment to reflexivity, and the recruitment of a facilitator outside the project team, supported mentors in reflecting critically on their role within this collaboration. The involvement of three sets of participants (mentors, schools, and government advisers) within the Schools of Ambition programme created a set of complex dynamics between different participants: the mentor and the school; the mentor and adviser; and between the school and adviser (Baumfield, Hulme and Menter 2009). The key challenge for partnerships lies in managing the interaction of the different modes of working, what has been described as the 'irregular heartbeat' of a partnership. Working in a longer-term project (2006–2010) allowed for growth in understanding as schools came on-stream in three successive tranches for a period of three years. Mentors accrued experience over time as they toggled between 'interventionist' and 'facilitative' roles (Grundy, Robison and Tomazos 2001).

Concurrent research in the UK (Baumfield 2001; McLaughlin and Black-Hawkins 2004) emphasises that if university–school research partnerships are to be viable then there have to be mutual benefits, reciprocity and a genuine coalition of interest. Whilst this is an obvious statement to make, it describes a situation that is difficult to achieve given the protean quality of partnership and the fact that amongst the partners there will be different understandings of research, its purpose and role, and not necessarily any single shared understanding of the concept of a school–university research partnership.

Our experience suggests that forging partnerships across institutional and professional boundaries requires constant consideration of the ends of partnership work, as much as the means. In reflecting on progress, it is important to consider the extent to which collaboration supports teachers in 'learning to ask different questions' (Harrington et al. 2006). The emphasis placed on problem posing at an early stage is informed by Spillane's (1999, 157) caution that research engagement can entail the translation of a will and capacity to learn about practice into a will and capacity to 'do reformers bidding'. From this perspective, school research networks might be seen to open up a space for participants to signal broad alignment with institutional goals, offering a new opportunity for 'creative conformity' (Hegarty 2000) rather than new forms of extended professionalism. Although opportunities arose for individual teachers to become engaged in research through Schools of Ambition, the focus of enquiry for some has not necessarily aligned with their own interests but on the requirement to evaluate particular elements of the school's transformational plan. Within some school structures, this was an unpromising start for partnership. In such circumstances, the tension between the evaluation and support roles of university mentors can become acute and the potential for building and sustaining research capacity through collaborative enquiry is diminished.

Developing an inquiry focus for a partnership can be a means of establishing parity and mutual interest (Baumfield and Butterworth 2007). Establishing a coalition of interest (Baumfield and McLaughlin 2006) around an inquiry also ensures that the outcomes of collaboration include learning. As Orland-Barak and Tillema (2006) have shown, whilst collaboration may have benefits these do not necessarily include the creation of appropriate conditions for learning. Cochran-Smith and Lytle (1993) describe focusing on practitioner inquiry as 'working the dialectic' as it has the potential to transform rather than simply add to what is already known in the academy about teaching and learning. Equity lies in the shared context for the inquiry and a critical factor here is the extent to which this is framed so as to pose questions that not only are of mutual interest to all of the participants, but which also have sufficient uncertainty and ambiguity to instigate the need to exchange ideas and interpretations from the perspectives of the different partners. As discussed earlier, this process requires time to establish relations of mutual trust and to build shared understandings of the purposes of collaboration. Working on an externally funded project, which sets conditions to which all the partners are subject, can provide such a space- and time-limited context (Baumfield and Butterworth 2007) and constitutes a challenge to the view that external funding can only be detrimental to partnerships (Miles 1978).

Carlone and Webb (2006) note that despite the well-intentioned involvement of university personnel, there seldom appears to be any disruption to the university model of support over multiple attempts at participation. The challenge of 'doing practitioner research differently' (Dadds and Hart 2001) continues to hold currency.

There has been a tendency among studies that have focused on 'teachers as researchers' to neglect the significance of participation in collaborative research partnerships for reciprocal professional learning. Attention is directed at teachers' development and outcomes for learners. It should be noted that mentors too work within the considerable constraints of a 'new academic professionalism' that has come to characterise work within the 'entrepreneurial university' (Nixon 2004). Further work might usefully address the challenges of the mentor role and the range of influences on different mentoring styles, such as biography, career trajectory, professional identity, institutional positioning and epistemology. This is pertinent given the recent emphasis on research, innovation and evaluation within the integrated professional development frameworks for teacher education, the move towards Masters-level components within postgraduate initial teacher education programmes, and the expanding provision for professional doctorates.

The Schools of Ambition mentor team included a mix of experienced teacher educators and education researchers from other backgrounds, and some had limited experience of school and classroom life. With respect to the impact on the professional learning of the university participants, while reflecting that at times the mentor role had often been a frustrating experience characterised by 'uncomfortable collaboration' (Menter and Hulme 2009), all judged it to be worthwhile. Involvement in the Schools of Ambition programme encouraged reflection on the value of supporting teacher research, the impact of partnership working within the wider context of university work, deliberation on what counts as research evidence in this context, and how it would be judged in terms of academic rigour.

The role of teacher educators is in transition. Research mentorship may be an increasing role for teacher educators, many of whom will be concurrently engaged in developing their own research profile. With their unique position in university faculties of education linking research and practice, teacher educators are well placed to contribute to capacity building through teacher enquiry. Opportunities for sustained engagement (focused on the collaborative identification of shared local 'problems', *co*-development (and alignment) of school curriculum, pedagogy and assessment, successive cycles of collaborative action research undertaken by co-enquirers) would support the development of capacity for (and with) teachers and teacher education. A significant development in this process, as articulated by Whitehead (2007), would be a move away from dominant conceptions of school–university collaboration that rely on the transitional metaphors of 'boundary crossing' towards the development of networks of 'complementary expertise'.

Note

1. The Research Support Team includes Alison Devlin, Dely Elliot, Stuart Hall, Moira Hulme, Kay Livingston, Kevin Lowden, Irene McQueen, Ian Menter (University of Glasgow); Norman Coutts, Fran Payne, Dean Robson, Jenny Spratt (University of Aberdeen); Donald Christie and Sanna Rimpilainen (University of Strathclyde).

References

Altrichter, H., and P. Gstettner. 1993. Action research: A closed chapter in the history of German social science? *Educational Action Research* 1, no. 3: 329–60.

Anderson, G.L. 1999. The politics of participatory reforms in education. *Theory into Practice* 38, no. 4: 191–5.

Anderson, G.L., K. Herr, and A.S. Nihlen. 1994. *Studying your own school: An educator's guide to qualitative practitioner research.* Thousand Oaks, CA: Corwin Press.

Audit Scotland. 2006. A mid-term report. A first stage review of the cost and implementation of the teachers' agreement *A teaching profession for the 21st century*, May.

Ball, S.J. 1987. *The micro-politics of the school.* London: Methuen.

Baumfield, V.M. 2001. *The north-east school based research consortium: Final report.* Newcastle upon Tyne, UK: University of Newcastle.

Baumfield, V.M., and A.M. Butterworth. 2007. Creating and translating knowledge about teaching and learning in collaborative school/university research partnerships. *Teachers and Teaching: Theory and Practice* 13, no. 4: 411–27.

Baumfield, V.M., and C. McLaughlin. 2006. Bridging and bonding: Perspectives on the role of the university in SUPER. In *Researching schools: Stories from a school–university partnership for educational research,* ed. C. McLaughlin, K. Black Hawkins, S. Brindley, D. McIntyre, and K. Taber, 132–46. London: Routledge.

Baumfield, V.M., M. Hulme, and I. Menter. 2009. Negotiating research relations in the Scottish Schools of Ambition: Supporting school self-evaluation through professional enquiry. In *Partnership in education,* ed. P. Masson and M. Pilo. Lille, France: The Book Edition.

Carlone, H.B., and S.M. Webb. 2006. On (not) overcoming our history of hierarchy: Complexities of university/school collaboration. *Science Education* 90, no. 3: 544–68.

Cochran-Smith, M., and S.L. Lytle. 1993. *Inside out: Teacher research and knowledge.* New York: Teachers College.

Cochran-Smith, M., and S.L. Lytle, eds. 2009. *Inquiry as stance. Practitioner research for the next generation.* New York: Teacher College Press.

Cochran-Smith, M., and K. Zeichner, eds. 2006. *Studying teacher education: The report of the AERA panel on research and teacher education.* Washington, DC: AERA and Lawrence Erlbaum Associates.

Craig, C.J. 2009. Teacher research and teacher as researcher. In *International handbook of research on teachers and teaching,* ed. L.J. Saha and A.G. Dworkin, 61–70. Boston, MA:Springer Science and Business Media.

Cruikshank, B. 1999. *The will to empower: Democratic citizens and other subjects.* New York:Cornell University Press.

Dadds, M., and S. Hart, eds. 2001. *Doing practitioner research differently.* London:Routledge.

Day, C. 2007. Ethical issues for consultants in complex collaborative action research settings. In *An ethical approach to practitioner research,* ed. A. Campbell and S. Groundwater-Smith, 42–61. London: Routledge.

Day, C., and M. Hadfield. 2004. Learning through networks: Trust, partnerships and the power of action research. *Educational Action Research* 12, no. 4: 575–86.

Department for Education and Employment. 2000. *Best practice research scholarships. Guidance notes for teacher applications.* Nottingham, UK: DfEE Publications.

Elliott, J. 2001. Making evidence-based practice educational. *British Educational Research Journal* 27, no. 5: 555–74.

Fielding, M. 2003. The impact of impact. *Cambridge Journal of Education* 33, no. 2: 289–95.

Foster, P. 1999. 'Never mind the quality, feel the impact': A methodological assessment of teacher research sponsored by the Teacher Training Agency. *British Journal of Educational Studies* 47, no. 4: 380–98.

Furlong, J. 2004. BERA at 30: Have we come of age? *British Educational Research Journal* 30, no. 3: 343–58.

Furlong, J., and A. Oancea. 2006. Assessing quality in applied and practice-based research in education: A framework for discussion. Review of Australian research in education: Counterpoints on the quality and impact of educational research. *Australian Educational Researcher* 6: 89–104.

Furlong, J., J. Salisbury, and L. Coombs. 2003. *Evaluation of best practice research scholarship programme.* London: DfES.

Grundy, S., J. Robison, and D. Tomazos. 2001. Interrupting the way things are: Exploring new directions in school–university partnerships. *Asia Pacific Journal of Teacher Education* 29, no. 3: 203–17.

General Teaching Council for Northern Ireland. 2005. *GTCNI reviews of teacher competences and continuing professional development.* Belfast, Northern Ireland: GTCNI.

General Teaching Council for Northern Ireland. 2007. *Teaching: The reflective profession.* Belfast, Northern Ireland: GTCNI. http://www.gtcni.org.uk/uploads/docs/GTCNI_Comp_Bmrk%20%20Aug%2007.pdf

General Teaching Council for Scotland. 2002. *Standard for full registration.* Edinburgh, UK: GTCS.

General Teaching Council for Scotland. 2006. *Standard for initial teacher education.* Edinburgh, UK: GTCS.

General Teaching Council for Wales. 2006. *A professional development framework for teachers in Wales.* Cardiff, UK: GTCW.

Hargreaves, A. 1994. *Changing teachers, changing times: Teachers' work and culture in the postmodern age.* London: Cassell.

Harrington, P., K. Gillam, J. Andrews, and C. Day. 2006. Changing teaching and learning relationships through collaborative action research: Learning to ask different questions. *Teacher Development* 10, no. 1: 73–86.

Hegarty, S. 2000. Teaching as a knowledge-based activity. *Oxford Review of Education* 26, nos. 3–4: 451–65.

Hillage, J.R., A. Pearson, A. Anderson, and P. Tamkin. 1998. *Excellence in research on schools.* London: DfEE.

HM Inspectorate of Education. 2006. *How good is our school? The journey to excellence.* Livingston, UK: HM Inspectorate of Education.

HM Inspectorate of Education. 2007. *Teaching Scotland's children: A report on progress in implementing 'A teaching profession for the 21st century'.* Livingston, UK: HM Inspectorate of Education.

Hulme, M., and I. Menter. 2008. Learning to teach in post-devolution UK: A technical or an ethical process? *Southern African Review of Education* 14, nos. 1–2: 43–64.

Hulme, M., D. Elliot, A. McPhee, and F. Patrick. 2008. *Professional culture among new entrants to the teaching profession. Report to the General Teaching Council for Scotland and the Scottish Government.* Edinburgh, UK: GTCS/Scottish Government.

James, M., and M. Worrall. 2000. Building a reflective community: Development through collaboration between a higher education institution and one school over 10 years. *Educational Action Research* 8, no. 1: 93–114.

James, R., and D. Egan. 2004. *Evaluation for the General Teaching Council Wales of the phase three professional development projects.* Bristol, UK: Tribal Education.

Kirkwood, M., and D. Christie. 2006. The role of teacher research in continuing professional development. *British Journal of Educational Studies* 54, no. 4: 429–48.

Lassonde, C.A., and S.E. Israel. 2008. *Teachers taking action.* Newark, DE: International Reading Association.

Lawn, M. 2004. The institute as network: The Scottish Council for Research in Education as a local and international phenomenon in the 1930s. *Pedagogica Historica* 50, no. 5: 719–32.

Learning and Teaching Scotland. 2003. *Focusing on curriculum flexibility in secondary schools: A paper for professional reflection.* Dundee, UK: Learning and Teaching Scotland.

Leitch, R. 2008. Capacity and quality in education research in Northern Ireland. In *Strategic forum for research in education, stimulus reports: England, Scotland, Wales, Northern Ireland,* 93–125.

Lowndes, V., and C. Skelcher. 1998. The dynamics of multi-organisational partnerships: An analysis of changing modes of governance. *Public Administration* 76, no. 2: 313–34.

McLaughlin, C., and K. Black-Hawkins. 2004. A schools–university research partnership: Understandings, models and complexities. *Journal of In-Service Education* 30, no. 2: 265–83.

McLaughlin, C., K. Black-Hawkins, S. Brindley, D. McIntyre, and K.S. Taber. 2006. *Researching schools: Stories from a schools–university partnership for educational research.* London: Routledge.

Menter, I. 2009. Teachers for the 21st century – what have we got and what do we need? In *Changing teacher professionalism. international trends, challenges and ways forward,* ed. S. Gewirtz, P. Mahony, I. Hextall, and A. Cribb. Abingdon, UK: Routledge.

Menter, I., M. McMahon, C. Forde, J. Hall, A. McPhee, F. Patrick, and A. Devlin. 2006. *Teacher working time.* Edinburgh, UK: Scottish Negotiating Committee for Teachers.

Menter, I., and M. Hulme. 2009. Teacher researchers in the UK: What are their needs? Some lessons from Scotland. In *Connecting inquiry and professional learning in education: International perspectives and practical solutions,* ed. A. Campbell, and S. Groundwater-Smith, 217–28. Abingdon, UK: Routledge.

Miles, M. 1978. *On networking.* Washington, DC: Centre for Policy Research, National Institute of Education.

Miller, L. 2001. School–university partnership as a venue for professional development. In *Teachers caught in the action: Professional development that matters,* ed. A. Lieberman and L. Miller, 102–17. New York: Teachers College Press.

Munn, P. 2008. BERA presidential address: Building research capacity collaboratively: Can we take ownership of our future? *British Educational Research Journal* 34, no. 4: 413–30.

Murray, J., A. Campbell, I. Hextall, M. Hulme, M. Jones, P. Mahony, I. Menter, R. Procter, and K. Wall. 2009. Research and teacher education in the UK: Building capacity. *Teaching and Teacher Education* 25, no. 7: 944–50.

Nixon, J. 2004. Education for the good society: The integrity of academic practice. *London Education Review* 2, no. 3: 245–52.

Orland-Barak, L., and H. Tillema. 2006. The 'dark side of the moon': A critical look at teacher knowledge construction in collaborative settings. *Teachers and Teaching: Theory and practice* 12,1: 1–12.

Ozga, J., and L. Walker. 1995. Women in educational management. In *Gender and changing educational management,* ed. B. Limerick and B. Lingard, 34–43. Sydney, Australia: Hodder.

Perry, C., L. Komesaroff, and M. Kavanagh. 2002. Providing space for teacher renewal: The role of the facilitator in school–university partnerships. *Asia Pacific Journal of Teacher Education* 30, no. 3: 243–57.

Prestage, S., P. Perks, and A. Soares. 2003. Developing critical intelligence: Tensions in the DfES model for best practice research scholarship. *Educational Review* 55, no. 1: 55–63.

Ravid, R., and M.G. Handler, eds. 2001. *The many faces of school–university collaboration.* Englewood, CO: Teacher Ideas Press.

Rönnerman, K., E. Furu, and P. Salo, eds. 2008. *Nurturing praxis: Action research in partnerships between school and university in a Nordic light.* Rotterdom:Sense Publishing.

Scottish Executive Education Department. 2004. *Ambitious, excellent schools: Our agenda for action.* Edinburgh, UK Scottish Executive.

Schön, D. 1983. *The reflective practitioner: How professionals think in action.* London: Temple Smith.

Sikes, P. 2006. Working in a 'new' university: In the shadow of the Research Assessment Exercise. *Studies in Higher Education* 31, no. 5: 555–68.

Spillane, J.P. 1999. External reform initiatives and teachers' efforts to reconstruct their practice: The mediating role of teachers' zones of enactment. *Journal of Curriculum Studies* 31, no. 2: 143–75.

Stoll, L., and K. Myers, eds. 1998. *No quick fixes: Perspectives on schools in difficulties.* London: Falmer.

Strategic Forum for Research in Education. 2008. Quality and capacity in UK education research. http://www.sfre.ac.uk/wp-content/uploads/2009/03/report-final-march-2009.pdf (accessed June 20, 2009).

Street, H., and J. Temperley. 2005. *Improving schools through collaborative enquiry.* London: Continuum.

Training and Development Agency. 2007. *Professional standards for teachers. Why sit on your career?* London: TDA. http://www.tda.gov.uk/upload/resources/pdf/s/standards_a4.pdf (accessed March 14, 2009).

Tooley, J., and D. Darby. 1998. *Educational research: A critique. A survey of educational research.* London: Ofsted.

Tripp, D. 1998. Critical incidents in action inquiry. In *Being reflexive in critical educational and social research,* ed. G. Shacklock and J. Smyth, 36–49. London: Falmer.

University of Glasgow. 2008. Research to support Schools of Ambition. Annual report. http://www.scotland.gov.uk/Resource/Doc/241691/0067162.pdf

Whitehead, J., ed. 2007. Collaborative approaches to preparing and developing effective teachers. An account of the joint UCET/HMI/SCET symposium held in Glasgow, March 27. *UCET Occasional Papers.* No. 16. London: UCET.

Scallops, schools and scholars: reflections on the emergence of a research-oriented learning project

Donald Gray[a], Archie Graham[a], Yvonne Dewhurst[a], Gillian Kirkpatrick[b], Lindsay MacDougall[a], Sandra Nicol[a] and Graeme Nixon[a]

[a]School of Education, University of Aberdeen, Aberdeen, UK; [b]Formerly University of Aberdeen, Aberdeen, UK

This article is based on the emergence of a small research group and its journey to enhance scholarly activity within a new school of education. While exploring a research-orientated learning project to determine what makes a beneficial school experience, the group comprising seven academics developed a way of working collaboratively. Narrative enquiry and hermeneutic analysis were used to develop descriptions and interpretations of the phenomenon from the perspective of the participants who in themselves were the researchers and also the researchers of the research process. Drawing on actor-network theory to explore the network of relationships, the pattern that emerged closely followed that described by Michel Callon in his study of the scallops of St Brieuc Bay. The analysis is presented and discussed to help understand the processes that contribute favourably to research capacity building in an academic institution.

Introduction

In his study of how marine biologists try to restock the St Brieuc Bay on the Normandy coast of France with scallops, Michel Callon (1986) defined four moments of translation, or the process of actors building a forum, or central network, that has some common goal and is worth pursuing. Translation is a concept central to actor-network theory (ANT), sometimes known as the sociology of translation and along with other elements of ANT can be used to examine and try to understand, processes or interactions that take place within a traceable network of human and non-human actors, or actants. Using Callon's four moments of translation as a heuristic to aid interpretation of both textual and oral accounts of a process we engage in self reflection on the emergence and development of a research group within a new university school of education.

Research as capacity building

This paper is concerned with the idea of research as capacity building, through a case study of the emergence and development of a small research group in a new school of education, in contributing to the further expansion of a scholarly community. The premise underlying the goal of a scholarly community within the context of this study is that the work completed by this research group would simultaneously facilitate and contribute to the professional development of each group member to engage with future research. Scholarship is defined by Shulman (1998) cited by Nicholls (2004, 30) as:

> …any activity of 'critical, systematic investigation in one or more fields and the submission of one's findings for criticism by professional peers and the public through published writings, lectures, or other modes of presentation'.

In addition Boyer's (1990) analysis of scholarship asserts four key forms (discovery, integration, application, and teaching) which can be used as a framework for classifying the various kinds of work undertaken by academics. A 'scholarship of discovery' can be viewed as being closely related to the traditional aim of research activity that captures both 'intellectual excitement' as well as knowledge production. The inclusion of the 'scholarship of integration' is in response to the realisation that there is a need to engage in interpretation of any knowledge that is produced. The 'scholarship of application' is most relevant to research in education and is defined as professional activity in practice and service. The final classification relates to the 'scholarship of teaching' and while considered to be a distinct category it is also permeates the other three forms.

Background

The case study examined here is set within the context of a recent merger between a college of education and a university. As has been common throughout Europe, and perhaps globally, many teacher education institutions, primarily separate colleges of education, have merged with higher education institutions to become faculties, or schools, of education. As a result of these mergers, staff within these institutions found themselves in situations where research, having previously been of a low, or lower, priority was now elevated to a position where it became a central requirement. Such was the case for the School of Education at Aberdeen, which was formed from the merger of the former Northern College and the University in 2001, with a subsequent move from the campus of the former college, to the campus of the main university in 2005. Northern College, Aberdeen, was the last of the colleges of education in Scotland to merge with a university.

The transition from a teaching dominated culture to one in which research was expected to play a more prominent role, was further emphasised by the award to the School of Education of two major projects, the Scottish Teachers for a New Era (STNE) initiative and the Inclusive Practice Project (IPP), both of which were required to use research informed processes in taking forward decisions about programme developments. This article focuses on the emergence and development of a small research group arising from the STNE initiative in the School of Education.

Scottish Teachers for a New Era

The STNE initiative is based on, although not aligned with, the Teachers for a New Era (TNE) initiative in the USA, which is largely funded by the Carnegie Corporation. STNE is jointly funded by the Scottish government and the Hunter Foundation. While the foundation of STNE is based on TNE it has to respond to the specific contexts of Scottish education and the requirements of initial teacher education in Scotland.

However, while it has developed in its own way it started with the same three key design principles (Scottish Executive Education Department 2003) for those institutions delivering teacher education in the USA TNE sites, which are: decisions driven by evidence; engagement with the arts and sciences; and teaching as an academically taught clinical practice profession. While there are historical and cultural reasons for these design principles, and there are differences in initial teacher education between Scotland and the USA, the principles provided the focus for discussion at the outset of the STNE initiative in the School of Education at Aberdeen. The early discussions in STNE resulted in the formation of theme groups charged with taking forward thinking in key areas and one of these was 'Communities for Learning'. We can for the purposes of this article take this to mean a group of people who share common values and beliefs and are together actively engaged in learning. The process examined in this article emerged from the Communities for Learning theme group.

Communities for Learning

The STNE Communities for Learning share many of the characteristics of Wenger's (1998) Community of Practice in that it defines itself along three dimensions:

- What it is about – its *joint enterprise* as understood and continually renegotiated by its members
- How it functions – the relationships of *mutual engagement* that bind members together into a social entity
- What capability it has produced – the *shared repertoire* of communal resources (routines, sensibilities, artefacts, vocabulary, styles, etc.) that members have developed over time (2)

The Communities for Learning was named such to reflect the focus on a central aspect of STNE, which was learning. The principle aim for the Communities for Learning theme group was to research terms such as 'communities for learning', 'partnership' and 'collaboration' and to investigate ways of supporting the range of participant voices in order to sustain the development of the STNE project and beyond. The theme group had responsibility for highlighting the importance of how we work together, to reflect on how we do this, and to monitor how this might have to change over time and in different contexts

The evolving nature and dynamics of the processes

The work of the theme group, while no longer formally constituted as originally conceptualised, continues and develops thinking in relation to the way in which groups, or associations, come together to take forward 'learning projects' (Graham and Gray 2007) or research in particular areas. Out of the initial meetings of the theme group a learning project emerged where a small number of staff embarked on an examination of what makes a beneficial school experience. Perhaps it is this idea of emergence that begins to take shape in the idea of developing research capacity: the context of institutional research being a dynamic system that is continuously changing, a network of relationships in which the links between aspects continuously strengthen and weaken depending on the interests, directions and actions of the participants. It was this aspect that began to surface within the group, an interest not only in the focus of the research being undertaken in itself, but also in the way in which the group came together, developed and moved forward.

The reading of the group, over a period of time has encompassed activity, complexity and actor-network theories, and there is a recognition of overlaps amongst these different theories from which we can draw on to inform our thinking. However, while the group continues to elaborate its thinking, and draws on other theories, the main focus of the current work has been informed by ANT, which was suggested as potentially providing a way forward. ANT was principally developed by two leading French scholars working in the field of science and technology studies, Michel Callon and Bruno Latour, as well as the British sociologist John Law and principally offered new insights into the study (Latour 1987, 2005; Callon 1986; Law 1992). A key feature of ANT is that it includes both human beings and non-human actors (such as tools and documentation), which together form a network of 'actants' to be studied, and the *relationality* amongst the different elements is key to understanding the network. The purpose of the research in both areas was therefore to describe, rather than predetermine, the networks that were emerging and thus, through exploring this relationality, we were able to reveal the fluidity, evolving nature and dynamics of the processes. It is this aspect that is the particular focus here – the group's own investigation into the process of their formation and way of working.

Thus, this particular piece of research might be described as a piece of reflective research on, and by, the group itself, a collective gathering of consciousness that externalised and analysed our own perceptions and experiences and those externalisations became the data through which the group developed an awareness of themselves as a group and also provided a model for the way in which such 'associations for learning' (Graham and Gray 2007) come together, carry through an activity for a particular purpose and finally disband or reorganise to take forward something new. This might be seen as an example of Boyer's (1990) notion of a 'scholarship of application'.

The composition of the group that comprises the subject of the case study here consisted of seven members of academic staff from the School of Education. All seven members had previously been employed as practising teachers in either the primary or secondary sector prior to making the transition into higher education. Only one was considered to have been an experienced researcher, having spent the previous 14 years in predominantly research environments engaged as a researcher on a number of varying types of research projects. The other six members of the group all professed to being novice researchers with little or no experience of research, any research having been conducted as a participant in a formal educational programme leading to some form of certification or qualification. Of the six 'novice' researchers two were male, four were female, two (one male and one female) coming from a background in secondary teaching and the remaining four from a background in primary teaching. Three of the group were in their thirties, one in their forties and the remaining three in their fifties, one of these being the experienced researcher. Two of the six novice researchers had recently embarked on part-time doctoral studies, one of these being the convener of the group. The convener of the group was not the experienced researcher.

Method

Having decided that ANT was a useful body of ideas to draw from in both the research being undertaken, and in analysing the process of the research undertaken it was necessary to then conduct an analysis of this process as it had unfolded, to develop descriptions and interpretations of the phenomenon from the perspective of participants, researchers and others.

The method used was that of narrative enquiry and hermeneutic analysis (Elliot 2005; Flyvbjerg and Sampson 2001) to develop descriptions and interpretations of the phenomenon from the perspective of the participants who in themselves were the researchers and also the researchers of the research process.

Step 1

The first step in this process was to record and describe the practices as events i.e. what happened, when it happened, where it happened and the circumstances under which it happened. 'This description of practices as events endures and gains its strength from detecting the forces that make it work'. (Flyvberg and Sampson 2001, 135).

To do this, two of the group compiled and analysed all the communications that had taken place amongst the group, essentially consisting of emails, but also notes taken at meetings. All the members of the group also agreed to be interviewed to gather perceptions and recollections of their engagement with the process. In order to do this it was necessary to engage an *outsider*, a member of the School of Education staff who had not previously been involved with the group, to conduct the interviews (see Appendix 1) and to provide a compilation of the findings.

Step 2

Following a hermeneutic process described by Flyvberg and Sampson (2001) the data, events and phenomena were scrutinised together with their connections with other data, events and phenomena. Thus, the transcripts were used for 'drawing out the logical relationships between members'. (Schostak 2002, 87).

Step 3

Individual practice is taken as the 'horizon of meaning' and this hermeneutic horizon was isolated and the researcher then 'attempts to understand the roles played by the practices studied in the total system of relations' (Flyvbjerg and Sampson 2001, 135), with no practice being seen as more valuable than another.

Step 4

The roles and relations in the total system of relations is then elaborated as a narrative for making sense of the experience. 'We begin with an interest in a particular phenomenon and develop descriptions and interpretations of the phenomenon from the perspective of the participants, researchers and others'. (Flyvbjerg. and Sampson 2001, 137).

Step 5

The participants, or actors, and their roles, functions and practices can then be analysed in relation to structures in terms of agency, 'not so that the two stand in an external relation to each other, but so that structures are found as part of actors and actors as part of structures' (Clegg et al. 2006, 378).

Results

At the time this research was initiated the 'data' consisted of the content of 64 email communications, notes from seven interviews compiled by the *outside* interviewer, the documentation from internal seminars, notes from meetings, working proposals and conceptualisations and presentations from earlier conferences.

The key events over time that occurred during the instigation, development and implementation of the research are elaborated and set beside the four moments of translation that Callon (1986) suggests take place during the construction of a forum involving a network of actors/actants. Our interpretation of these four steps in relation to the work of the group is outlined and described in Table 1.

Callon (1986) describes a four-step process whereby an organisation can learn from how actants align their interests and the function of other actants together in a chain. The four moments of translation ('Problematisaton', 'Interessement', 'Enrolment' and 'Mobilisation') merit some further elaboration here.

The first step is referred to as Problematisation and can be stimulated by a Community of Practice, a bottom-up or top-down initiative, or an individual interest. A problem is defined in such a way that others can recognise the problem as being relevant to them, but in the process the first set of actors indicate that they have the means of resolving the shared problem. In this case study, problematisation occurred at the first meeting, which had been an open meeting to explore issues of common interest with respect to Communities for Learning. The session drew on the expertise of one of the participants to draw out ideas and thinking around the theme. This was later revealed to be a very engaging activity which resulted in a sense of common purpose among the group, although the specific goal and course of action had yet to be determined.

The second stage or moment, Interessement, involves engaging professional curiosity. At this stage the learning agenda can be negotiated and roles and responsibilities identified for mutual benefit and collaborative working. Within the research group we have described this as engaging professional curiosity whereby the participants extend their level of interest by committing to a set of goals and a course of action. Following the initial meeting, those who were interested met again to discuss their areas of common interest and converged on a specific focus, in this case the Professional Graduate Diploma in Education (PGDE) students' school experience. However, it was only in subsequent meetings that this focus, and the use of ANT as a body of ideas to examine the school experience, became more evident. So the process that might be equated to interessement took place over a number of meetings, drawing again on particular people from within the group who took responsibility for doing the major reading and conceptualisation around ANT, and then sharing this with the group.

The third stage in the process, Enrolment, is where the participants carry out the agreed course of action. As the group explored and deepened their thinking the project took shape and individuals took on clearly defined roles. In this case the group consolidated specific roles and activities that collectively contributed to the overall project. There is a fourth and final stage, Mobilisation, which emerges when practice and ways of working become embedded. As the research progressed the group could be said to

Table 1. Identification of key events compared with Callon's (1986) four moments in translation.

Event	Description	Moment of translation
Initial invitation	Open invitation to staff to explore and discuss communities for learning and to identify areas of common interest.	Problematisation
Identification of the 'problem'	Further meeting and focussed discussion to identify the 'problem'.	
Elaboration of a theoretical framework and literature review	Initial reading and elaboration of a possible theoretical framework undertaken by particular individuals.	Interessement
Elaboration of roles and responsibilities	Consolidation of the theoretical framework through group discussion and implications for research design.	Enrolment
Data gathering and analysis	Methodology elaborated and instruments devised. Specificity of roles and responsibilities within the group elaborated to undertake particular tasks.	
Conference presentation	First overall reporting from individuals stemming from their particular roles and responsibilities in the overall process.	Mobilisation
Writing	Sharing and elaboration of ideas and conceptualisation to elaborate on the conference presentation and paper articles for peer reviewed journals.	

have arrived at Callon's fourth step, Mobilisation, which is characterised by each constituency in a project being represented by one or two individuals who report on the progress being made towards the shared goals. Of specific interest in this process is the temporary nature of the network and the assertion that at any point it can collapse if one or more of the actants withdraws from the interest alignment. In this case it transpired that two of the original group did withdraw, one because of a move overseas and the other because of commitment to other areas of involvement. However, their particular roles had been more prominent earlier in the process and so there was little impact on the overall progress of the group in taking the project further as the overall working of the group had become more distributed across a range of individuals in the group, so if there was a withdrawal it was possible for that to be accommodated within the group at this stage.

The mobilisation of the group continues with other papers being prepared on the actual study itself, but it is recognised that this particular grouping, or association, for this particular study is approaching the end of its life and will at some point in the near future dissolve in its current form, perhaps to disappear altogether, or to reconfigure with another point of focus. Further to the elaboration of the key moments in the unfolding of the project, more detailed analysis of the interviews, communication and documentation was undertaken and a number of themes emerged. These are described in the following sections.

Sense of purpose

From the outset all those who subsequently joined and stayed with the group expressed a clear sense of purpose, of common interest, that had been stimulated and supported by the opening workshop session where a member of the group with particular interest and expertise in using thinking skills techniques had involved those present in a process of exploration around the theme of Communities for Learning.

The interviews conducted with the members of the group all suggested a clear sense of common purpose which was meaningful to the group:

> The problem was identified early on (and was of) mutual interest to everyone involved. (Interviewee 6, notes)
>
> Felt positive about it. (Interviewee 3, notes)
>
> Interested because of it going to be a team effort. (Interviewee 4, notes)
>
> It was interesting because it was contextualised and sat in course developments. (Interviewee 6, notes)

Group dynamics

There was an overwhelming sense of positive group dynamics with each person bringing something different. At the early stages, some in the group had reservations about their research capabilities, but trusted in others and developed their own capacity over time:

> The group dynamics worked well together. (Interviewee 4, notes)
>
> People didn't feel it was a chore. It was interesting and worth pursuing and the group stayed engaged. (Interviewee 5, notes)

> Why I continued? I felt very comfortable in the group and didn't feel inhibited in any way. (Interviewee 6, notes)
>
> I was accepted as part of the team even although my own research was limited to individual small-scale research (Interviewee 7, notes)
>
> Truly collaborative… feel responsibility to other members of the team. (Interviewee 3, notes)

The latter comment highlights the importance of commitment as an aspect. The idea of commitment to the group emerged as a key element and links to Callon's third moment of Enrolment. Here we have individuals taking on roles with a professional responsibility to contribute to the group as a whole.

Roles and responsibilities

From the beginning some of the group had expressed reservations about their expertise and relied on others to take things forward in the early stages. However, as the group gelled and began to create a 'safe space' for discussion where all viewpoints were respected, confidence developed and members of the group took on roles and responsibilities to progress aspects of the project:

> Didn't get to do enough reading at the beginning. Difficult to engage with. (Interviewee 6, notes)
>
> My role changed from observer/listener, a passive supporter of ideas, to participant and making a contribution. (Interviewee 3, notes)

Drawing from expertise

Members of the group recognised that individuals within the group brought differing experiences and expertise. Early in the process, those individuals with more experience and expertise took on more of the roles, with this gradually changing as greater understanding and confidence developed. However, it was also evident that those who had less experience, or familiarity with the topic, or process played a key role in asking important questions:

> Asymmetrical group – people of different experiences. (Interviewee 1, notes)
>
> 'A' [has]… good idea of theory… and keeps focus (Interviewee 6, notes)
>
> Those with less knowledge – played an important role questioning/asking for clarity. Space for everyone and everyone contributed. (Interviewee 1, notes).

Regular communication

Communication was essential in keeping members of the group informed of progress, as not all members could attend all meetings. As such there had to be times when meetings were convened when there was a window of opportunity that allowed most or many of the group to meet. However, in general the group met regularly at convenient times with those unable to attend kept addressed of developments and thinking:

> After each weekly session – emailed to let everyone know about progress. (Interviewee 1, notes).
>
> Regular meetings but at a pace which allowed everyone to participate. (Interviewee 1, notes)

> Constantly kept in the loop. (Interviewee 2, notes)
>
> In most cases meetings have been at dates and times that have suited me. (Interviewee 7, notes)

Leadership

While the group dynamics played an important part in the cohesiveness of the group, leadership of the group was clearly a key factor in maintaining the momentum and work of the group, with the original convener of the group emerging as a natural leader, recognised and respected by the rest of the group. It was through the consistency of approach, regular communication and organisation of meetings that the group stayed together as a fairly cohesive group over a long period of time:

> 'A' a good leader, he enables all to participate. (Interviewee 6, notes)
>
> Need people like 'A' to keep things going. (Interviewee 5, notes)
>
> Natural leader – looked towards him for direction. (Interviewee 3, notes)
>
> Had 'A' not held the threads together, we may not have continued. (Interviewee 4, notes).

Sharing

The sharing of experiences and expertise was seen to be an important element in the group dynamics. While individuals continued to develop and learn, they also found they were able to contribute more by drawing on their own experiences and networking outwith the group to keep it on task:

> Enjoyed the debate and seeing other perspectives and how this can enhance personal group thinking. (Interviewee 7, notes)
>
> Latterly sharing experience rather than gaining. Within sub-group [I've] been able to help analyse data for research purposes. (Interviewee 4, notes)

Emphasis on maintaining relationships

One of the clear messages that came through from the interviews was the sense of a collaborative, trusting and cohesive group. There was a sense that this just happened to be serendipitous but also that the particular mix of individuals, experiences and expertise helped the group to move forward:

> The dynamics of the group are very important, specific individuals encourage others – good reputation. (Interviewee 3, notes)
>
> Trust and integrity was evident in the group. (Interviewee 3, notes)
>
> It was very collaborative, but constructing our own understanding. (Interviewee 6, notes)
>
> Feeling valued (and) Being part of a wider research team. (Interviewee 7, notes)

Personal development

While the group convened through a preliminary mutual interest, which was then elaborated to form the focus of a research question, and it was the pursuit of an answer to the question that held the focus of the group, individuals also benefited in tangible ways which were recognised by all members of the group:

> Working on collaborative project has helped develop confidence in undertaking research. (Interviewee 6, notes)
>
> The literature review process has been very rewarding. Enhanced my own research. (Interviewee 2, notes)
>
> Learning about how to be part of a wider research group and how discussion can spark off/feed ideas. (Interviewee 7, notes)
>
> I ultimately wanted to improve my research profile. I was very interested and enthusiastic about research and became determined because of this. (Interviewee 4, notes)
>
> Leading project, learnt a lot. (Interviewee 1, notes)

However, while the overall comments from the interviews painted a very positive picture of the experience, there were aspects that participants found more uncomfortable and problematic. A few of the participants felt that the adoption of the ANT framework had been a little premature and had not been fully discussed, as well as finding the concept somewhat hard to grasp:

> I would have liked ANT to be raised at the beginning instead of thinking skills. (Interviewee 4)
>
> I am confused about ANT and its application to the problem. (Interviewee 2)
>
> The whole project was based on Actor-Network Theory, but didn't have to fully understand it to be able to contribute and make a difference. (Interviewee 3)
>
> I feel that it is still a loose framework for me that is only partially clothed. (Interviewee 7)

However, while these comments might suggest that the group members were not fully conversant with the ideas drawn from ANT a further period of writing and reflection has taken place since these questions were asked. All those participating in the subsequent writing and discussions would now agree that they are comfortable with the concept as their understanding has developed more fully.

Another aspect raised was the way in which participants took on, or were allocated, roles and responsibilities with, in some cases, these being allocated because of time pressures of an imminent conference presentation:

> We didn't spend enough time articulating roles and responsibilities, lucky that we worked well as a team (Interviewee 4)
>
> SERA [Scottish Educational Research Association] conference was an afterthought and people were allocated randomly to ensure we submitted in time. (Interviewee 4)

While this interviewee suggests that presenting at the conference was an afterthought, it can be said that it was also seen as an opportunity, which, while coming a little premature for some members of the group provided a forum for public scrutiny of the work in progress.

Discussion

So what is the significance of this reflection on a group's research activity? In some respects it only has real meaning for those involved in it, as a means to examine the establishment and development of a particular group, for a particular purpose over a given period of time. As Haggis (2009), citing Davis and Sumara (2006, 55) and referring to 'structure determinism' states:

> As discussed above, even two apparently similar systems will be emerging out of quite different initial conditions, past histories, and presently-connected other systems; likewise, apparently similar sets of initial conditions, histories and present constellations may give rise to two very different systems.

If we accept this then we have to ask the question what can be learned from an analysis of a case study of this type. The answer could well be that it is not the case in itself that provides any kind of answer, or model, but rather the way in which a case can study itself to try to look for aspects that indicate meaningful and fruitful ways of working in a specific context, in a situation that brings with it its own particular history. Even within the structure of the School of Education, it is apparent that there is a constant dynamic of groups coming together to take forward an area of apparently common interest. Some of these groups survive and thrive, but others falter and fade. By conducting an analysis of the way in which a successful group has emerged from a common background and taken forward a particular initiative, which is not driven by any external pressure but rather from a common shared interest, we can perhaps begin to identify some principles that, while providing no guarantee of success as every group is made up of different combinations of individuals, are more indicative of successful engagement than others.

Perhaps what is of greatest significance in this case is, however, the process of engagement with the research activity and the developing dialogue that took place over a period of time. Participants found themselves in a space in which they felt supported and secure, with a group of people with differing experiences and expertise, but all of whom had a common interest and desire to develop their own thinking. Engagement with theory became an essential component in the process, and such engagement deepened participants own thinking and developed an understanding of their own role within that theoretical framework. The constant iterative process of dialogue and refinement provided a series of recursive loops for individuals to revisit and refine their own thinking, at the same time contributing to the greater understanding of the group as a whole. Schostak (2002, 86), referring to the hermeneutic process and mirroring also a complexity framework, describes this as 'a spiral that moves between individual… and the greater whole of which he or she is a part'.

In terms of research capacity building we can look at this process as the cultural role of research in which research has a 'practical impact if it helps practitioners to acquire a different understanding of their practice' (Biesta 2009, 3). Here Biesta cites Dutch sociologist Gerard De Vries (1990) who describes two ways in which research can be useful for practice. On the one hand it can produce 'technical' or 'instrumental' knowledge, what De Vries refers to as the technical role of research, or it can have a cultural role in which, as a result of the research, 'we may see new and different opportunities for action and improvement. The cultural role of research is thus no less practical than the technical role; it is just a *different* way in which research can be useful for educational practice' (Biesta 2009, 3).

In the same paper, presented at a Teaching and Learning Research Programme event on 'Methodological Development, Future Challenges', Biesta (2009, 8) goes on to discuss methodology and theory and suggests that 'whereas a lot has been invested in design, method and methodology, relatively little attention has been paid to the other main "tool" of educational researchers – the tool called "theory"'. In the case study presented here, one of the key developments in the process was the observable engagement of 'novice' researchers beginning to engage with theory in an educational context. While the data analysed for this paper were gathered at a specific point of time, just before the group was about to make a presentation at the annual conference of SERA (Dewhurst, MacDougall and Nicol 2007; Graham and Kirkpatrick 2007; Gray and Nixon 2007), the preliminary grappling with theory had already taken place with ANT and has since gone on to interrogate and compare with Activity Theory in relation to the piece of research that was undertaken by the group.

If we return to the central theme of this article with respect to research capacity building, we can frame this here in relation to learning. Research capacity building involves learning about research, learning to do research and all the different strands that are so intricately entwined in this concept of research. The group, or association, that formed here emerged from within a community for learning, with an identified common interest which they elaborated, refined and pursued. In the process of doing so they learned collectively as a group, but they also learned individually developing in areas that they had had little experience of. Through the process of engagement with research they grappled with theory in a way that they had had little experience of before and they learned more about the culture of research.

We see here, then, the potential capacity for 'novice' researchers to strengthen any initial fragile link with research by gathering together for a common purpose and a strengthening of these fragile (research) links in terms of engagement with the group, contributions which developed and strengthened over time. As Latour (1997) states, 'Strength does not come from concentration, purity and unity, but from dissemination, heterogeneity and the careful plaiting of weak ties'. Also, from the narratives produced by the participants, we can identify a number of aspects that contributed to the successful and sustained engagement of the group with the research that they undertook. It required a common understanding of the 'problem', which was arrived at by the group collectively and not imposed from outside, there was mutual trust and respect for the different experiences and expertise brought to the group by individuals, recognising also that even those with little prior research expertise could make valuable contributions. A 'safe space' was created that enabled engagement with the issues and for individuals to feel secure and supported in that space. Thus, what could clearly be identified in this small case study was the emergence of a 'culture' of research and scholarly activity within the group. This culture evolved and developed through collaborative and collegiate activity amongst a group of individuals with a common interest, mutually agreed through discussion and reflection and with continuous and deepening engagement with theory. Perhaps then, what can be learned from this is that research capacity building consists of multiple dimensions and there may be a role for the technical and methodological training kind of capacity building, but that probably the most effective form of capacity building is the reflection on practice in practice in a 'safe' space where individuals trust and feel trusted, where dialogue is concerned with understanding and refinement of theoretical ideas and how these relate to oneself as well as to the study 'out there'. There needs to be a constant moving between perspectives with the acknowledgement of multiple viewpoints and the space to become a researcher as well as a teacher, which we would see as a further example of Boyer's (1990) 'scholarship of application'. In addition, important to the group was the idea of learning and, as such, research is learning and becomes a key component of teaching as the two have moved from being seen as separate activities (as either/or), to becoming two elements of the central focus, which is learning:

> Scholarship is not an esoteric appendage; it is at the heart of what the profession is all about. All faculty, throughout their careers, should themselves, remain students. As scholars they must continue to learn and be seriously and continuously engaged in the expanding intellectual world. This is essential to the vitality and vigour of the undergraduate college. (Boyer 1987, 131)

References

Biesta, G. 2009. Educational research, democracy and TLRP. Invited lecture presented at the TLRP event 'Methodological Development, Future Challenges', March 19, in London. http://www.tlrp.org/conference/2009/docs/gertbiesta.pdf (Accessed 19 April 2009).

Boyer, E. 1987. *College. The undergraduate experience of America, The Carnegie Foundation for the Advancement of Teaching.* New York: Harper and Row.

Boyer, E. 1990. *Scholarship reconsidered. Priorities of the professoriate.* Princeton, NJ: Princeton University Press.

Callon, M. 1986. Some elements of the sociology of translation: Domestication of the scallops and fishermen at St Brieuc Bay. In *Power, action and belief: A new sociology of knowledge,* ed. J. Law, 196–223. Sociological Review Monograph 32. London: Routledge and Kegan Paul.

Clegg, S., C. Hardy, T. Lawrence, and W.R. Nord, eds. 2006. *The Sage handbook of organization studies.* London: Sage.

De Vries, G.H. 1990. *De ontwikkeling van wetenschap.* Groningen, The Netherlands: Wolters-Noordhoff.

Dewhurst, Y., L. MacDougall, and S. Nicol. 2007. Actor-network theory and the beneficial school experience. Presentation at the SERA annual conference 2007 symposium, 'Actor Network Theory, Associations for Learning and The School Experience in Scottish Teachers for a New Era', November 22–24, in Perth, UK.

Elliott, J. 2005. *Using narrative in social research.* London: Sage.

Flyvbjerg, B., and S. Sampson. 2001. *Making social science matter: Why social inquiry fails and how it can succeed again.* Cambridge, UK: Cambridge University Press.

Graham, A., and D. Gray. 2007. Developing communities for learning. Presentation at the AERA annual conference 2007 symposium, 'Scottish Teachers for a New Era: Examining Change, Collaboration, Ways of Working, Assessment and Initial Teacher Education', April 8–12, in Chicago, IL.

Graham, A., and G. Kirkpatrick. 2007. Communities for practice, associations for learning and the learning project. Presentation at the SERA annual conference 2007 symposium, 'Actor Network Theory, Associations for Learning and The School Experience in Scottish Teachers for a New Era', November 22–24, in Perth, UK.

Gray, D., and G. Nixon. 2007. Actor network theory: A theoretical framework for examining the school experience. Presentation at the SERA annual conference 2007 symposium, 'Actor Network Theory, Associations for Learning and The School Experience in Scottish Teachers for a New Era', November 22–24, in Perth, UK.

Haggis, T. 2009. Beyond 'mutual constitution': Looking at learning and context from the perspective of complexity theory. In *Rethinking contexts for learning and teaching,* ed. R. Edwards, G. Biesta, and M. Thorpe, 44–60. Abingdon, UK: Routledge.

Latour, B. 1987. *Science in action: How to follow scientists and engineers through society.* Milton Keynes, UK: Open University Press.

Latour, B. 1997. The trouble with Actor-Network Theory. In 'Om aktor-netvaerksteroi. Nogle fa afklaringer og mere end nogle fa forvikinger'. *Philsophia* 25, nos. 3–4: 47–64. http://www.bruno-latour.fr/poparticles/poparticle/p067.html

Latour, B. 2005. *Reassembling the social, an introduction to Actor-Network Theory.* Oxford, UK: Oxford University Press.

Law, J. 1992. Notes on the theory of the actor network: Ordering, strategy and heterogeneity. Centre for Science Studies, Lancaster University. http://www.lancs.ac.uk/fass/sociology//papers/law-notes-on-ant.pdf (accessed April 8, 2009).

Nicholls, G. 2004. Scholarship in teaching as a core professional value: What does this mean to the academic? *Teaching in Higher Education* 9, no. 1: 29–42.

Schostak, J.F. 2002. *Understanding, designing and conducting qualitative research in education.* Buckingham, UK: Open University Press.

Scottish Executive Education Department. 2003. Developing teachers, increasing pupil gains: A new pilot programme to further develop teaching as a valued and recognised profession in Scotland. Invitation to tender document. Scottish Executive Education Department and the Hunter Foundation.

Wenger, E. 1998. Communities of practice: Learning as a social system. *Systems Thinker* 9, no. 5. http://www.ewenger.com/pub/pubpapers.htm (accessed April 8, 2009).

Appendix 1. Questions asked of members of the group during interview

1. Describe your experience of participating in the Learning Project from its initial conception to the present.
2. Can you identify reasons for your continuing participation in this Learning Project and provide supporting examples?
3. To what extent did participation in the Learning Project contribute to your professional development? Please provide some examples to illustrate your response.
4. This Learning Project claims to draw from ANT as its underlying approach to collaboration i.e. identification of a shared 'problem' that is of mutual interest the identification of negotiated goals and, roles and responsibilities within the subsequent project implementation of roles, responsibilities and the agreed course of action. To what extent do you think this claim can be justified? Can you provide examples to support your response?
5. If you could rewind time how do you think things could have been done differently?
6. Having participated in this Learning Project what future applications, if any, do think there are for this approach to collaborative working?

The TEG bibliography: having knowledge and using it – next steps?

Karl Wall[a], Anne Campbell[b], Ian Hextall[c], Moira Hulme[d], Marion Jones[e], Pat Mahony[c], Ian Menter[d], Jean Murray[f] and Richard Procter[g]

[a]Department of Psychology and Human Development, Institute of Education, London, UK; [b]Carnegie Faculty of Sport and Education, Leeds Metropolitan University, Leeds, UK; [c]Roehampton University, London, UK; [d]Department of Curriculum Studies, University of Glasgow, Glasgow, UK; [e]Faculty of Education, Community and Leisure, Liverpool John Moores University, Liverpool, UK; [f]Cass School of Education, University of East London, London, UK; [g]Freelance consultant, UK

This paper acknowledges and refers to the recent online release and updating of the Teacher Education Group (TEG) bibliography. It offers a brief summary of how and why it was felt necessary to create the resource, what it covers and how it can be used. Broader issues of what skills and prior understanding a naïve user of its various search facilities might need are raised. It is suggested that additional pedagogically focused tools will need to be developed and suggests what these might be. Finally the paper argues that for the Bibliography to be used more widely, further development work will be needed, focused around the provision of user tools and support materials.

What is the 'TEG bibliography'?

The Teacher Education Group (TEG) bibliography is an online, annotated bibliography. It contains hundreds of articles focused on teacher education research in the UK. These articles have been drawn from peer-reviewed journals, published in a wide range of UK-based journals. The TEG resource is intended to provide a starting point for new and existing researchers as they explore the teacher education literature. To support this exploratory emphasis, the resource can be searched in a variety of ways. The bibliography also aims to support beginning researchers in teacher education as they develop their research skills. A range of other resources support the use of the bibliography as an annotated database. These include embedded links to resources via thematic walkthroughs. These walkthroughs serve as a stimulus for those wishing to find out about a specific topic.

Background to the creation of the TEG bibliography

The origins and processes around creating the TEG bibliography have been reported in detail in earlier publications by the TEG (Murray et al. 2008, 2009). These accounts focused on how two key issues were addressed: what was to be understood by 'teacher education research'; and second, what type of review was to be undertaken. For the first of these a broad definition of what constituted teacher education research was adopted, which took account of the range of perspectives offered by the members of TEG itself and the impetus of each of the funding organisations underwriting the project and their various constituencies. These were the British Educational Research Association, the University Council for the Education of Teachers and ESCalate, the Subject Centre for Education, within the Higher Education Academy and the Teaching and Learning Research Programme (TRLP) overall. Emerging from these different views, 'Teacher education' was taken to include initial teacher education (ITE) and the continuing professional learning/development of teachers within the primary, secondary and post-compulsory sectors in the UK. It therefore embraced:

- ITE
- Induction
- Early professional learning
- Continuing professional development (CPD)
- Career-wide professional learning
- Relevant research on policy (as well as practice)

Given its target users (teacher educators and those they worked with and supported) the 'review' also needed to include research that addressed the particular challenges of becoming a teacher educator. These issues were further informed by a need to draw on and connect with existing literature reviews of teacher education, taken broadly, in and relevant to the UK jurisdictions of England, Wales, Scotland and Northern Ireland. Having defined what was meant by 'teacher education research' the next step was to identify the sources from which the peer-reviewed literature at the heart of the bibliography would be taken. The final list of journals (taking account of recent updates to the database for April 2009) is shown in Table 1.

Looking at this list with the broad definition given earlier in mind, it is clear that jurisdiction coverage is apparent; that the different phases of education as research contexts have been included; that dimensions of teacher professional development and work context have been addressed, as has the issue of teacher practice and its underlying theoretical aspects. Broader cultural and pedagogical areas have been indicated, including policy as well more specific issue dimensions such as gender and disability. Equally a research and development focus is evident and, within the criteria noted previously, European and international journals focusing on the UK have been included. In terms of face-validity the list is comprehensive in that it recognisably covers a non-curriculum subject-based overview of teacher education research. What then would a 'review' mean across this range of journal titles, in this context?

Creating the TEG bibliography – the underlying 'review'

The TEG, along with Walliman (2005), took the view that the process of engaging with a particular literature involves taking a view of and about that literature. This necessarily produces a nuanced (and so arguably biased and certainly selective) account of that literature. If this decision then informs the inclusion or exclusion of a particular piece of literature, what is 'in' or 'out' further filters, but also helps to define, what a 'comprehensive' account of the field in question might be.

To ensure that no relevant paper might be missed by the TEG, a systematic checking of all the papers in each issue of the identified journals (over the period 2000–2009)

Table 1. The Teacher Education Group bibliography: journals featuring in the bibliography.

Journal (n=43)
British Educational Research Journal
British Journal of Educational Studies
British Journal of Sociology of Education
Cambridge Journal of Education
Curriculum Journal
Disability and Society
Educational Action Research
Educational Philosophy and Theory
Educational Research
Educational Research and Evaluation
Educational Review
Educational Studies
European Journal of Educational Research
European Journal of Teacher Education
Gender and Education
Higher Education Quarterly
Higher Education Review
International Journal of Educational Research
International Journal of Research and Method in Education
International Studies in Sociology of Education
Irish Educational Studies
Journal of Curriculum Studies
Journal of Education and Work
Journal of Education for Teaching
Journal of Education Policy
Journal of Further and Higher Education
Journal of In-Service Education
Journal of Post Compulsory Education
Journal of Vocational Education and Training
Management in Education
Mentoring and Tutoring: Partnership in Learning
Oxford Review of Education
Pedagogy, Culture and Society
Professional Development in Education
Research in Education
Research in Post-Compulsory Education
Research Papers in Education
Scottish Educational Review
Teacher Development
Teachers and Teaching
Teachers and Teaching: theory and practice
Teaching and Teacher Education
Welsh Journal of Education

Note: As of April 2009.

was undertaken. Papers relating to the topics identified in the definition given earlier were retained. From the same definitions, a list of topic categories was identified. A second list of categories identifying the research methodologies/methods used in the retained studies was also made. These two sets of categories (core topics and core methodologies) were then systematically applied to all of the papers from the original journal search. The papers from the original trawl through the journals thus ended up annotated according to the topic(s) they addressed and the methodology(s)/method(s) they employed. The abstracts of these papers and their associated topic and methodology/method annotations formed the basis of the content of the searchable database that became the TEG bibliography. A fuller account of the processes involved is given in (Murray et al. 2008, 2009).

The TEG had already envisaged that the mapping task which led to the creation of the bibliography itself was about more than creating an annotated bibliography: as a resource it was intended also to generate new insights into the field when used by more experienced researchers. This captures what Hakim (2000, 21) may have meant when suggesting that 'a comprehensive review can become a research project yielding substantive information in its own right'.

What emerged from these considerations was the view that the creation of the TEG resource would be based around a bounded literature search aimed at generating a comprehensive bibliographical source: the TEG bibliography. Just as a real map does not contain all the possible topological information potentially available about a particular area, but does contain key positional and feature information, so the TEG bibliography aimed to be comprehensive. It identified the main mountains and valleys, but did not seek to give the reader information about specific paths through those mountains: that was to be the job of the walkthroughs and other pedagogic guides.

Creating the bibliography involved balancing a need to identify what was available (a question of coverage and constituency) on the one hand and on the other hand wanting what was identified to be comprehensive, compendious and representatively diverse and indicative.

Using the TEG bibliography

The TEG bibliography is essentially a very long list of peer-reviewed and published abstracts. There are a variety of ways in which this resource can be searched or filtered. Each abstract is complete with title, year of publication, author(s) and journal source. When accessed online, these are shown as they would appear in the journal that published the original paper. In addition, each abstract has been categorised according to a range of topics (see Table 2) identified by the TEG as noted earlier.

Each abstract in the data base has also been categorised on the basis of the methodology and methods employed in the study it reports. A list of these categories is shown in Table 3.

The utility of the TEG bibliography

The potential utility of the bibliography lies in its coverage of contemporary teacher education-related research, broadly defined. The bibliography's comprehensive online search facilities allow users to select items by topic, research method, author,

Table 2. Core topic categories in the Teacher Education Group bibliography.

Curriculum and assessment
Equity issues
Ethical issues
National context
Partnership
Professional learning
Regulatory frameworks and policy
TE (teacher education) professional development

Table 3. Core method categories in the Teacher Education Group bibliography.

Action research
Case study
Content analysis
Interviews
Large-scale study
Literature review
Longitudinal
Mixed methods
Political economy
Practice-based
Qualitative
Quantitative
Quasi-experimental
Questionnaire
Reflection
Small-scale
Survey

and year of publication or journal title and cover the period 2000–2009. At the end of each search, users can then download a citation list, which also includes the abstract for each article. It is also possible to go directly from a specific abstract to the actual journal paper providing a user's institution has a subscription to the journal in question.

Users can apply their own search strategies to the way sources are filtered within the bibliography. A single category may be used, for example, searching by year of publication. Alternatively multiple categories may be used in, for example, combining author name, year of publication and journal name. The effect of these more complicated searches is to produce a shorter, more focused and specific list of results.

Users who are less certain of what they are looking for and want a broader search approach can start by using the methodology and core topic filter options. Here a user might want to approach a particular research interest from the perspective of how it has previously been investigated – the range of strategies and approaches used. So, for example, users could search for all entries that used interviews as a research tool by selecting this method in the 'core methods' option. Equally the prospective researcher might have a theme in mind, such as professional learning; this can be selected through the 'core topics' option. For users who want to search for something not identified by either a topic focus or methodology approach, a free word search option is also available.

For beginning researchers this resource provides a starting point to a literature review, using peer-reviewed, academic UK-based journals. It can also save time for busy professionals whether as established researchers, new researchers, tutor-researchers, tutors or as students. The bibliography's specific and comprehensive search categories allow users to do a first sweep of the literature and also more detailed and specific searches. In so doing, established areas of research can be surveyed and under-researched areas identified (Menter et al. in press). Users, particularly beginning researchers, will find the resource especially helpful as they explore a range of different research approaches and methodologies when preparing for research activity.

By combining different search strategies and topics, users can explore an educational issue from a range of different perspectives. They can look comparatively at the ways different research strategies have been used and how this has related to research outcomes and produced different forms of research evidence.

There are, however, limitations built into the bibliography (reported in detail in Murray et al. 2008, 2009) as part of the process of making its creation practicable in the time available; for example, it does not specifically include curriculum subject-specific areas, such as science education, although these may be included by default within the core topics. The bibliography is also restricted to the UK context, but the references attached to each article often serve as links to research published in journals not included in the bibliography.

Broader issues around using the TEG bibliography: naïve users and their needs

The TEG envisaged that prospective users of the bibliography would lie along a continuum running from those with no prior research experience to those that were more experienced researchers. It was also important that the resulting resource would draw on the research activity of the existing education community, the same community that the resource would ultimately serve. In this community much teacher education research is carried out by educators themselves. These practitioner/researchers were thus likely to be working as teachers and managers of pre- and in-service provision. Developing research-capacity in order to strengthen these communities and to enhance student and teacher learning quality had been identified as critical in a range of previous research (Cochran-Smith and Zeichner 2006; Menter, Brisard, and Smith 2006).

Researchers using the TEG bibliography would need access to resources that could develop research skills. They would also need opportunities to put those newly acquired or developing skills into practice. Because of the range of potential users, any such resources or tools would need to be flexible and adaptable. They would also need to be easy to distribute both geographically to particular institutions and within institutions, to particular individuals. Being freely available online would address these needs. It was further hoped that making this research available would promote the development of communities of users who would, in turn, encourage the further development of different sets of illustration and extension material, also as free educational goods (Mahony and Menter 2006).

Users of the TEG bibliography would necessarily limit and make explicit, the nature of any links among the sources they identify through their choice of search terms, categories and filtering characteristics. However, implicit associations among the research items returned by their query might also be present.

The act of assembling a list of abstracts as a result of an introductory search does not necessarily establish a connection with prior research and its context. Users would also likely need to establish how the development of ideas found in their search findings might relate to their research question. It was thus also important for users to be able to 'demonstrate how the research being reported relates to previous research and… how it gives rise to particular issues, problems and ideas that the current research addresses' (Denscombe 2005, 293). The TEG bibliography does not do this, nor does it support researchers in developing the skills needed to make it possible; it was not intended to.

As the bibliography cannot be a tutor in any conventional sense, the development of walkthroughs, as structured introductions to particular areas of research, were proposed as a way of giving an initial context to different areas of research. These would allow users to relate their choice of abstracts to broader areas of the literature. Alternatively the creation of timelines linking particular aspects, theories, approaches or debates in the field might be constructed. These would offer users a further form of mapping focusing on the relationships between different articles as links in a relational chain of ideas. However, to date such timelines have not been attempted.

Another type of issue arises from what a naïve user of the resource might make of some of its potential outputs. For example, a count of how many items were included from each year covered by the bibliography produces the following result (Table 4).

Looking at Table 4 it is apparent that different years have apparently contributed different numbers of articles to the database, with those in the last three years (2006–2008) contributing markedly more. How can this be?

The rate of production of new material in the field does not *a priori* have to be constant; different journals have different publication cycles in any one year; different issues or types of journal (a review-based journal versus an individual research-style journal) may offer more or fewer papers; special issues may focus upon particular themes, which in turn may have created a focus group of relevant articles. On the other

Table 4. The Teacher Education Group (TEG) bibliography: number of items by year of publication.

Year of publication	Number of items
2000	40
2001	30
2002	43
2003	26
2004	30
2005	45
2006	72
2007	81
2008	79

Note: As of April 2009 there were 446 items in the TEG bibliography.

hand there might have been an increased focus on the issues forming the substantive focus of the bibliography, not least that arising from the TRLP itself. How would the naïve user make sense of these possibilities?

These observations alone suggest that for a naïve user of the bibliography there is a need for a broader contextualising account of the nature of journal publication, the process of paper submission and the basis of selection for publication. A research-experienced tutor might supply this but where that tutor, lacking research experience themselves, is the person in need of the tutoring, where does that support come from? Colleagues in a research-active setting would ordinarily help (and there would likely be existing training provision in place as well). But in a setting where research is not established, the resource itself might well need to offer that support and induction into the research literature and its exploration. Some of these issues are being addressed in a related project, the Teacher Education Research Network (TERN) project and have been introduced by Murray et al. in a recent article (2009).

TEG bibliography users will, it is assumed, be able to infer that the increase or decrease of identified articles in a particular year does not necessarily indicate a trend (perhaps teacher education research-related work was not the most frequent in 2004 – other issues may have held centre stage?). It is also assumed that users will realise that what is shown in the bibliography speaks only about what was included and not what was excluded, or why particular work was thought not to be relevant. This health warning, which may need to be made more explicit in the bibliography, links to issues of how the bibliography might be used in metric-based assessments of research activity level or research worth (Murray et al. 2008, 468–79).

Turning to Table 5 for a further example, the number of articles categorised by particular core topic category, raises further issues. The naïve user might immediately be stuck by the categories themselves and their relative frequency as they appear in the bibliography.

First, the categories are broad. They clearly focus on professional and teacher educator developmental issues but also take account of policy, jurisdictional and context informing issues. It is also apparent that specific items must be categorised in more than one way. This should tell the user straight away that it is unlikely that a particular item in the bibliography will be one-dimensional in its potential focus. This

Table 5. The Teacher Education Group (TEG) bibliography: number of items by core topic classification.

Core topic category	Number of items
Curriculum and assessment	148
Equity issues	77
Ethical issues	52
National context	367
Partnership	110
Professional learning	380
Regulatory frameworks and policy	256
TE (teacher education) professional development	52

Note: As of April 2009 there were 446 items in the TEG bibliography; the same item could be categorised under one or more core topic headings.

should also indicate the need for a careful consideration of any search strategy the user might have in mind.

Again, for an experienced user the need for such a strategy would be obvious. For someone new to the task it would be less so and there would need to be advice on how to go about this. At present there is no such guidance associated with the bibliography. Where would the naïve user get help to understand how to plan such a strategy? Discussing the use of the resource with the institutional librarian or again with another, more experienced colleague might be a solution. But this makes assumptions about the availability of library staff and access to experienced researchers. Once again a further pedagogic tool offering help in this respect may be needed.

Table 5 also signals another issue for the user of the bibliography – the comparative lack of equity and ethical categorisations. Here the low figure represents a real lack of attention to these issues evident in the materials in the database (Menter et al. in press). This lack of literature was also apparent during the journal review process, as material addressing these issues was remarkably scarce in the journals examined. This sits oddly with the knowledge that research planning (and ethical approval processes themselves) usually requires prospective research to be considered from an ethical point of view (Murray et al. 2008).

In a further example, (see Table 6) the user would need to differentiate between methodology and method as a way of breaking down the long list of core method categories reported.

Inspection of Table 6 raises some interesting questions, even allowing for the fact that the same piece of research might well have been categorised as qualitative,

Table 6. The Teacher Education Group (TEG) bibliography: number of items by core method classification.

Core method category	Number of items
Action research	35
Case study	83
Content analysis	100
Interviews	227
Large-scale study	112
Literature review	138
Longitudinal	38
Mixed methods	102
Political economy	100
Practice-based	137
Qualitative	185
Quantitative	38
Quasi-experimental	3
Questionnaire	129
Reflection	268
Small-scale	194
Survey	53

Note: As of April 2009 there were 446 items in the TEG bibliography; the same item could be categorised under one or more core method headings.

longitudinal, using interviews and analysed by content analysis and, thus, multiply categorised. The very low level of quantitative studies is striking, even when taking into account the possibility that 'mixed methods' may signal a quantitative element. Is this perhaps linked to the relatively greater incidence of 'small-scale' studies (defined as involving fewer than 100 participants) compared with 'large-scale' studies (greater than 100 participants)? The dividing line between small and large being needed here to avoid using narrower number ranges and so multiplying the number of categories. What in a research study constitutes small and large? Or is it linked to the low incidence of longitudinal studies where a quantitative element might be anticipated as large bodies of data accumulated over time? Large-scale research is usually expensive – perhaps the dearth of quantitative research reflects the costs associated with using a larger sample base? Exploring each of these possible interpretations and the extent to which they are real, would be difficult for the naïve researcher, new to interpreting and analysing search-related data. Pedagogic issues abound when the potential use of the bibliography moves beyond the simple downloading of search outputs.

Next steps in developing the TEG bibliography?

The range of issues raised in the last section of this paper signal a broader issue about how a naïve user of the bibliography might progress beyond simple information gathering. Looking across the incidence of the various categories in the database, one might ask how the new researcher is to make sense of the information available to them. They could consult a research methods text (Robson 2002), but this, while advising on types of methodology and specific methods, will not be able to address broader questions (in this instance, about the nature of the field and why particular strategies are adopted over others). The bibliography cannot do this and was not intended to do so. The task undertaken by the TEG was to construct a comprehensive, structured aggregation of instances of previous research; however, a pedagogic element remains necessary if such a link between instances of research and the field are to be bridged. Who should provide that pedagogic activity for the new researcher? Should not the institution that requires a teacher educator to be research-active support that possibility by supporting research training for that aspiring researcher? Does there not, therefore, need to be an institutional-level engagement and commitment to resources such as the TEG bibliography as part of the development of practice-located and -relevant research training?

The initial, and so far limited, monitoring of how the bibliography is being accessed or used does not suggest institution-level awareness or engagement – notwithstanding the four well-attended and oversubscribed dissemination events already held by the TEG, the conference presentations and published papers and presentation to various groups. It may be argued that while developing the bibliography has been an important first step, for it to be used and useful, there now needs to be a second step. This involves the funded development (working with potential users) and dissemination, of a series of pedagogic strategy 'guides' (Wall, Murray and Jones 2009) to support new users and, through such support, to develop users' research skills. These strategies need to reflect how a new researcher might begin and carry through the research process. These might include for example:

- Gaining an overview of the field
- Targeting particular aspects of the field

- Developing a research focus
- Developing a research question
- Identifying themes in the literature and exploring them
- Identifying methodologies as search design strategies and their implications
- Examining how particular instruments – survey or interview, for example – are used, why, in what context and for what purpose
- How is research literature organised or presented?
- What informs the drawing of conclusions?

Underneath these are the strategies and activities that permit the use of the TEG bibliography to support such investigations, the prior knowledge and skills that are needed to interrogate a literature database. This might include, for example: identifying initial research terms; how to frame and run a search strategy; how to read critically an abstract (and full paper) or how to extract meaning from different forms of data.

The TEG bibliography, even with an increased number of walkthroughs as guided commentaries on particular aspects of the field, cannot reasonably be expected to provide this pedagogic support. To make the resource actually useable in practice will need the provision of further 'How to'-type support. This was and is beyond the scope of the TEG as originally founded. For those organisations that originally funded and supported the project, a second step beckons.

References

Cochran-Smith, M., and K. Zeichner, eds. 2006. *Studying teacher education: The report of the AERA panel on research and teacher education.* Washington, DC: AERA and Lawrence Erlbaum Associates.

Denscombe, M. 2005. *The good research guide: For small-scale research projects.* Maidenhead, UK: Open University Books.

Hakim, C. 2000. *Research design: Successful designs for social and economic research.* London: Routledge.

Mahony, P., and I. Menter. 2006. TLRP on-line research capacity building resources initiative. A request for support from BERA Council meeting. Internal memo. Presented to the BERA Council Meeting, 14 November 2006

Menter, I., E. Brisard, and I. Smith. 2006. *Convergence or divergence?: Initial teacher education in Scotland and England.* Edinburgh: Dunedin Academic Press.

Menter, I., A. Campbell, I. Hextall, M. Hulme, M. Jones, P. Mahony, J. Murray, R. Procter, and K. Wall. in press. Teacher education research in the UK: the state of the art. *Swiss Review of Education.*

Murray, J., A. Campbell, I. Hextall, M. Hulme, M. Jones, P. Mahony, I. Menter, R. Procter, and K. Wall. 2008. Mapping the field of teacher education research: Methodology and issues in a research capacity building initiative in teacher education in the United Kingdom. *European Educational Research Journal* 7, no. 4: 459–74.

Murray, J., A. Campbell, I. Hextall, M. Hulme, M. Jones, P. Mahony, I. Menter, R. Procter, and K. Wall. 2009. Research and teacher education in the UK: Building capacity. *Teaching and Teacher Education* 25, no. 7: 944–50.

Robson, C. 2002. *Real world research: A resource for social scientists and practitioner-researchers.* Oxford, UK: Blackwell.

Wall, K., J. Murray, and M. Jones. 2009. The TEG resource: Initial evaluation and possible/ emerging pedagogic strategies for its use as a capacity building resource. Paper presented at the 5th Annual ESCalate ITE Conference, 15 May, at Glydwr University, Wrexham.

Walliman, N. 2005. *Your research project.* London: Sage.

Index

An environmentally friendly book printed and bound in England by www.printondemand-worldwide.com

PEFC Certified

This product is from sustainably managed forests and controlled sources

www.pefc.org

PEFC/16-33-415

MIX

Paper from responsible sources

FSC® C004959

www.fsc.org

This book is made entirely of sustainable materials; FSC paper for the cover and PEFC paper for the text pages.

#0409 - 071014 - C0 - 246/174/8 - PB